Just Listen 'n Learn
GERMAN

Second Edition

Ruth Rach

General editor, Brian Hill

Series advisers

Janet Jenkins
Duncan Sidwell
Al Wolff

PASSPORT BOOKS
a division of *NTC Publishing Group*
Lincolnwood, Illinois USA

Acknowledgements

My thanks to everybody in Germany who helped me recording this course, especially to the Ulm tourist office, and to **Deutsche Bundesbahn,** and **Deutsche Bundespost** for letting me use some of their original material. I would also like to thank my editor at Pan Books, Ursula Runde.

Tape production: Gerald Ramshaw, Claire Woolford
Acting: Michael Wolf, Lutz Liebelt, Sabine Michael
Book Design: Gillian Riley
Illustrations: Rowan Barnes-Murphy and Taurus Graphics
Photo credits: Ruth Rach, pages 13, 63, 65, 66, 91, 131, 123, 135
German Tourist Office, London, pages 26, 142, 165
Mary Glasgow Publications, pages 29, 47, 49, 51, 61, 105, 189
Inter Nationes, pages 44, 31, 89, 145
Presse-Bild-Poss, pages 40, 41, 35, 93, 103, 109, 147, 205
Munich Tourist Office, pages 68, 69, 95
Berlin Tourist Office and Landesbildstelle, pages 169, 195
Swiss National Tourist Office, London, page 157
German Embassy, page 189
Chris Fairclough, page 117

Note on the Accompanying Recorded Material

The *Just Listen 'n Learn* Language Programs are available in either audiocassette or compact disc formats. References in this book to the taped or recorded material apply equally to the audiocassettes and compact discs.

Also available
Just Listen 'n Learn German PLUS

1996 Printing

This edition first published in 1993 by Passport Books,
a division of NTC Publishing Group, 4255 West Touhy Avenue,
Lincolnwood (Chicago), Illinois 60646-1975 USA.
Originally published by Pan Books ® by Ruth Rach
and Brian Hill, 1993, 1982. All rights reserved. No part of
this book may be reproduced, stored in a retrieval system,
or transmitted in any form or by any means, electronic,
mechanical, photocopying or otherwise, without the prior
permission of NTC Publishing Group.
Manufactured in the United States of America.

67890 ML 987654

Contents

How to use this course

Following this course will help you to understand, speak and read most of the German you are likely to need on holiday or business trips. The course is based on recordings made in the Federal Republic of Germany, mainly in and around the city of Ulm in a region called **Schwaben** (Swabia). You will hear ordinary German people in everyday situations. Step by step you will learn first to understand what they are saying and then to speak in similar situations yourself.

Before producing the course we talked to many people about why and how they learn languages. We know how important it is for learning to be (a) enjoyable and (b) useable. There is not much point in knowing all the complex rules of German grammar if you are unable to ask for a beer. You will find a grammar section in each unit, but its main function will be to actually help you to understand and use the language.

General hints to help you use the course

- Have confidence in us! Real language is complex and you will find certain things in every unit which are not explained in detail. Don't worry about this. We will build up your knowledge slowly, selecting only what is most important to know at each stage.
- Try to study regularly, but in short periods. 20–30 minutes each day is usually better than 4 hours once a week.
- To help you learn to speak, say the words and phrases out loud whenever possible.
- If you don't understand something, leave it for a while. Learning a language is a bit like doing a jigsaw or a crossword; there are many ways to tackle it and it all falls into place eventually.
- Don't be afraid to write in your book and add your own notes.
- Do review frequently. (There are revision/review sections after every three units.) It also helps to get someone to test you – they don't need to understand German.
- If you can possibly learn with somebody else you will be able to help each other and practice the language together.
- Learning German may take longer than you thought. Just be patient and above all don't get angry with yourself.

Suggested study pattern

Each unit of the course consists of approximately thirteen pages in the book and around ten minutes of tape. The first page of each unit will tell you what you are going to learn, and you will also find our *study guide*. The study guide tells you the best way (we think) to tackle a unit. As you progress with the course you may find that you evolve a method of study which suits you better. That's fine, but we suggest you keep to our pattern at least for the first three units, or you may find you are not taking full advantage of all the possibilities offered by the material.

The book contains step-by-step instructions for working through the course: when to use the book on its own, when to use the cassette on its own, when to use them both together, and how to use them in each case. On the cassette our presenter Michael Wolf will guide you through the various sections. Here is an outline of the study pattern proposed.

Dialogues

Listen to the dialogues, first without stopping the tape, and get a feel for the task ahead. Then go over each dialogue or suggested group of dialogues in conjunction with the vocabulary and the notes. You should get into the habit of using the PAUSE/STOP and REWIND buttons on your cassette recorder to give yourself time to think, listen to sentences a number of times, and repeat them after the speakers. Don't leave a dialogue until you are confident that you have at least understood it.

Key words and phrases	Study this list of the most important words and phrases from the dialogues. If possible, try to learn them by heart. They will be practiced in the rest of the unit.
Practice what you have learned	This section contains a selection of listening exercises which are to focus your attention on the most important language in the unit. To do them you will need to work closely with the book. You will for instance often be asked to listen to a piece on tape and then fill in answers or tick off boxes in the book. Or you will be asked to write an exercise and then check the answers on the cassette. Again, use your PAUSE/STOP and REWIND buttons to give yourself time to think.
Grammar	At this stage in a unit things should begin to fall into place and you are ready for the grammar section. If you really don't like grammar you will still learn a lot without studying this part, but most people quite enjoy finding out how the language they are learning actually works and how it is put together. In each unit we have just selected one or two major grammar points.
Read and understand and *Did you know?*	In these sections you will be encouraged to read the kind of signs, menus, brochures, and so on you may come across in Germany. You will also be given some practical background information on all the German speaking countries, although we shall be concentrating mainly on the Federal Republic.
Your turn to speak	Finally back to the cassette for some practice in speaking the main words and phrases which you have already heard and had explained. The book only gives you an outline of the exercises, so you are just listening to your cassette recorder and responding. Usually you will be asked to take part in a conversation where you hear a question or statement in German, followed by a suggestion in English as to how you might reply. You then give your reply in German and listen to see if you were right. You'll probably have to go over these spoken exercises a few times before you get them right, and you will probably use your PAUSE/STOP and REWIND buttons a lot.
Answers	The answers to all the exercises (except those given on tape) can be found on the last page of each unit.

At the back of the book

At the back of the book there is a reference section which contains:

Symbols and abbreviations

If your cassette recorder has a counter, set it to zero at the start of each unit and then fill in these boxes with the number showing at the beginning of each dialogue. This will help you to find the right place on the tape quickly when you want to wind back.

♦ This indicates a key word or phrase in the dialogues.

m.	masculine	sing.	singular
f.	feminine	pl.	plural
n.	neuter	lit.	literally

The German language

Each language has its own peculiarities and its own character. Here are a few points to remember when learning German.

- there are 3 words for 'the' in German: **der** (for masculine nouns), **die** (for feminine nouns), **das** (for neuter nouns)
- all nouns are spelled with a capital, e.g. **der Mann** (the man), **die Frau** (the woman), **das Kind** (the child)
- dots on the letters a, o, u indicate an Umlaut: **ä, ö, ü**. These letters don't exist in English. You'll hear them being pronounced in Unit 1.
- **ß**. This letter stands for a double 's' (ss) and is pronounced like the 's' in 'some'.
- Apart from **ä, ö, ü** and **ß** German uses the same letters as the English alphabet, but the pronunciation is often different. The best way of finding out about pronunciation and picking up the right intonation is by listening to and copying the speakers on the cassette, all of whom are native Germans.
- German is a highly inflected language, i.e. the endings of words often change depending on whether a noun is masculine, feminine or neuter, singular or plural, etc. For the beginner this can be very confusing, and so we don't give rules for every ending or change of ending. We give general guidelines and select the most important features for description in the grammar section. These endings are relatively unimportant for making yourself understood – it's more important to get the main part of the word right.

1 Talking about yourself

What you will learn

- some different ways of saying 'hello'
- to introduce yourself and your family
- to ask people's names and where they're from
- to spell your name

and you will be given some information about how to address people when you meet them for the first time.

Before you begin

Below you will find a short *study guide*. It will take you through the unit step by step – from understanding the gist of the recorded dialogues to speaking your first sentence in German. Take your time, and if you haven't understood everything rewind your tape and listen again.

The dialogues at the beginning of each unit are of conversations which the course author, Ruth Rach, had with a wide variety of different people in Germany. Sometimes the same people appear in several dialogues but mostly you will meet new people from dialogue to dialogue and unit to unit. This will develop your ability to *follow the gist* of all kinds of spoken German right from the start and will prepare you for hearing German in Germany without panicking because you can't understand every word or because people have slightly different tones or accents.

Study guide

To help you keep a check on your progress, tick off the study guide list as you complete the tasks in the unit.

	Dialogues 1–3: listen straight through without the book
	Dialogues 1–3: listen with the book and study one by one
	Dialogues 4, 5: listen straight through without the book
	Dialogues 4, 5: listen with the book and study one by one
	Dialogues 6–8: listen without the book one by one
	Dialogues 6–8: listen with the book and study in detail
	Dialogue 9: listen with the book, several times
	Learn the *Key words and phrases*
	Do the exercises in *Practice what you have learned*
	Study the *Grammar* section and do the *Grammar* exercise
	Do the exercise and the puzzle in *Read and understand*
	Read *Did you know?*
	Do the exercises in *Your turn to speak*
	Listen to all the dialogues once again straight through

Dialogues

1 *Mrs Oswald introduces Mrs Rach and Mr Schmid to each other*

Frau Oswald Frau Rach, und Herr Schmid.
Herr Schmid Guten Tag, Frau Rach.
Frau Rach Grüß Gott, Herr Schmid.

♦ **Frau** Mrs
♦ **und** and
♦ **Herr** Mr

2 *Hermann introduces his wife and his baby son Robert*

Hermann Das ist meine Frau, und dies ist mein Sohn Robert.
Robert ablllllrlll!
Ruth Tag, Robert.
Hermann Sag mal was!
Robert äääääähhhhh!!

3 *Ruth gets to know Mr and Mrs Vollmert*

Frau Vollmert Guten Tag, mein Name ist Vollmert.
Ruth Guten Tag. Und Sie sind Herr Vollmert?
Herr Vollmert Richtig! Guten Tag.

richtig (that's) right

4 *Ruth asks Mr Gräter his name. He also introduces his wife*

Ruth Grüß Gott.
Herr Gräter Grüß Gott.
Ruth Wie heißen Sie?
Herr Gräter Alfons Gräter
Ruth Mhm . . .
Herr Gräter Meine Frau, Anneliese Gräter.
Ruth Aha. Guten Tag.
Frau Gräter Grüß Gott.
Ruth Grüß Gott.

1 ♦ **guten Tag** literally means 'good day.' This is the most common form of greeting in Germany, often shortened to just **Tag.** *Note:* in German you will find that many words begin with a capital letter – all nouns (words which could be preceded by 'a' or 'the' e.g. the/a day – **der/ein Tag**), proper names, names of countries, and the first words in a sentence.

grüß Gott literally greet (you) God. This is the South German way of greeting someone, and many Swiss and Austrian people prefer **grüß Gott** to **guten Tag.** The two dots over the 'u' in **grüß** are called an *Umlaut.* You will also find dots over 'a' and 'o' (ä, ö) in some words. The *Umlaut* changes the sound of the letters – listen out for the pronunciation on tape. The ß is really a double s (ss) and sounds like the s in '<u>s</u>ome'. The Germans call it *scharfes s* (sharp s). You can write **ss** instead of ß e.g. **grüss Gott.**

2 ♦ **das ist meine Frau** this is my wife. **Frau** can mean wife, woman, and Mrs.

♦ **dies ist mein Sohn** this is my son. Unlike the English *this* and *that* **dies** and **das** are more or less interchangeable. Hermann might just as well have said **dies ist meine Frau und das ist mein Sohn.** By the way if you are a woman and would like to introduce your husband, you say

♦ **das ist mein Mann** (**Mann** =husband, man). *Note:* you use **mein** for introducing a male person (**mein Sohn, mein Mann** my son, my husband) and **mein<u>e</u>** for a female person (**meine Frau** my wife).

sag mal was! say something!

3 **mein Name ist** my name is. A common introductory phrase. Note that you just add your surname – no title, e.g. **mein Name ist Rach.**

und Sie sind . . . and you are . . . **Sie** meaning 'you' is always spelled with a capital.

4 ♦ **wie heißen Sie?** what's your name? (lit. how are you called? **wie** = how)

aha meaningful grunt i.e. I see.

Alfons Gräter another *Umlaut*, this time an ä – **Gräter.**

5 *Cornelia, on the train from London to Cologne, answers a few questions*

Ruth	Guten Abend.
Cornelia	Guten Abend.
Ruth	Wie heißen Sie?
Cornelia	Cornelia Lämmermeier.
Ruth	Frau oder Fräulein?
Cornelia	Fräulein.
Ruth	Und wo wohnen Sie?
Cornelia	In Rottenacker bei Ehingen.
Ruth	Aha. Und woher kommen Sie jetzt im Moment?
Cornelia	Aus London, also aus England.

bei near
Rottenacker }
Ehingen } two towns in Southwest Germany
♦ **jetzt** now
im Moment at the moment

6 *Mr Marks tells Ruth that he's English – and a few more things*

Ruth	Sind Sie aus München?
Mr Marks	Nein, ich bin Engländer.
Ruth	Ah! Sie sind aus England. Sind Sie aus London?
Mr Marks	Ja.
Ruth	Sind Sie auf Geschäftsreise, oder sind Sie auf Urlaub?
Mr Marks	Nein. Ich wohne hier.
Ruth	Arbeiten Sie hier?
Mr Marks	Ja.
Ruth	Und wo?
Mr Marks	Hier an der Universität.

♦ **ja** yes
♦ **nein** no

7 *Two little boys by the river Danube – what are their names and where are they from?*

Ruth	Grüß Gott.
Hussein	Grüß Gott.
Ruth	Wie heißt du?
Hussein	Ich heiße Hussein Ichaltschin.
Ruth	Woher kommst du?
Hussein	Aus der Türkei.
Ruth	Ah, aber du sprichst gut deutsch.
Hussein	Ah ja.
Ruth	Grüß Gott. Wie heißt du?
Eliot	Grüß Gott. Ich heiße Eliot Fernando.
Ruth	Woher kommst du?
Eliot	Aus Portugal.
Ruth	Ihr seid wirklich international!
Eliot	Mhm.

5 ♦ **guten Abend** good evening. Equally important are
  ♦ **guten Morgen** good morning and
  ♦ **gute Nacht** good night.

  ♦ **Frau oder Fräulein?** Mrs or Miss? **Fräulein** literally means 'little woman'.
    In written German you find the abbreviations **Fr.** and **Frl.** for **Frau** and
    Fräulein. The *Umlaut* ä in combination with 'u' (äu) is always
    pronounced 'oy' (as in 'boy').

  ♦ **wo wohnen Sie?** where do you live? (literally 'where live you?' – there is no
    equivalent of the English 'do' in German here). **Wo** = where.

  ♦ **woher kommen Sie?** where do you come from? (**woher** = where from)

  ♦ **aus London, also aus England** from London, that is from England. Watch
    the word **also** – it does not mean 'also' but 'that is to say' or 'I mean'.

6 ♦ **sind Sie. . .?** are you. . .? (**Sie sind** = you are)

  ♦ **ich bin Engländer** I am English (lit. I am Englishman).
    A woman would have said **ich bin Engländerin** (see Unit 2 p. 31)

  ♦ **auf Geschäftsreise** on business.

  ♦ **auf Urlaub** on holiday.

  ♦ **ich wohne hier** I live here.

  ♦ **arbeiten Sie hier?** do you work here? Questions are easy to form in
    German. The word order in a sentence is normally like this:
    Sie arbeiten hier (you work here), but in a question it changes round like
    this: **arbeiten Sie hier?** (literally 'work you here?')

  an der Universität at the university.

7 **wie heißt du?** what's your name? There are two ways of addressing a
    person in German, **Sie** and **du**. You have come across **wie heißen Sie?**
    before, but when talking to children and good friends you always use **du**
    e.g. **wie heißt du?**

  woher kommst du? where do you come from? **Kommst** is the **du**-form of
  kommen (to come). You'll find all about verb forms in Unit 2.

  aus der Türkei from Turkey. You use **aus** to state which country or town
  you come from.

  aber du sprichst gut deutsch but you speak good German (**sprichst** from
  sprechen = to speak).

  aus Portugal from Portugal.

  ihr seid wirklich international! you are really international! As she is
  talking to the two boys together, Ruth now has to use the plural form of **du**
  which is **ihr** (**ihr seid** = you are, see *Grammar* section for full details).

8 *The shop assistant asks Ruth for her name and address*

Shop assistant	Wie ist Ihr Name bitte?
Ruth	Rach. R – a – c – h.
Shop assistant	Und Sie wohnen? Hier? In. . .?
Ruth	Fischergasse 17.
Shop assistant	Ja. In Ulm?
Ruth	In Ulm.
Shop assistant	Danke schön.

9 *Little Anne learns the alphabet*

Ruth	a, b, c, d	*Anne*	n
Anne	a, b, c, d	*Ruth*	o, p
Ruth	e, f, und g	*Anne*	o, p
Anne	e, f, und g	*Ruth*	q, r, s, t
Ruth	h, i, k, l	*Anne*	q, r, s, t
Anne	h, i, k, l	*Ruth*	u, v, w
Ruth	m, n, o, p	*Anne*	u, v, w
Anne	n, n, o, p	*Ruth*	x, y, z
Ruth	m, n, o, p	*Anne*	. . .z
Anne	n, n, o, p	*Ruth*	x, y, x
Ruth	m!	*Anne*	x, y, z
Anne	m	*Ruth*	Jetzt kann ich das Abc
Ruth	n!	*Anne*	Jetzt kann ich das Abc

8 ♦ **wie ist Ihr Name?** what's your name? This phrase is used at least as often as **wie heißen Sie?** Note that **Ihr** (your) is spelled with a capital – just like **Sie** (you).

und Sie wohnen? and you live? As in English, the upward lilt at the end indicates it's meant as a question.

♦ **hier. . .? in. . .?** here. . .? in. . .?

Fischergasse 17 17, Fisherman's Alley. A **Gasse** is an alleyway or narrow street. The German word for 'street' or 'road' is **Straße.** You'll often come across **Hauptstraße** (High Street) or **Bahnhofstraße** (Station Road). When saying or writing your address the number should always come *after* the name of the street.

in Ulm in Ulm.

♦ **danke schön** thank you, often shortened to simply **danke**. The usual response to **danke** is **bitte** – you're welcome;

♦ **bitte** also means 'please'. – Note the *Umlaut* ö in **schön**.

9 **jetzt kann ich das Abc** now I know the abc.

Note that Ruth forgot one letter – **j**, pronounced 'yot' (like the English word 'yacht').

Little Anne

Key words and phrases

Here are the most important words and phrases which you have either met
in the dialogues or which have been introduced in the notes. You should
make sure that you know them before you go on to the rest of the unit as
you will need them for the exercises to follow. You could practice by
reading them aloud.

Herr	Mr
Frau	Mrs; wife
Fräulein	Miss
Guten Tag	Hello; good day
Guten Morgen	Good morning
Guten Abend	Good evening
Gute Nacht	Good night
Das/dies ist. . .	This is . . .
meine Frau	my wife
mein Mann	my husband
mein Sohn	my son
Wie heißen Sie?	What's your name?
Wie ist Ihr Name?	
Ich heiße. . .	My name is. . .
Mein Name ist. . .	
Woher kommen Sie?	Where do you come from?
Ich komme aus (London)	I come from (London)
Sind Sie aus. . .	Are you from . . .
München?	Munich?
England?	England?
(Ja/nein,) ich bin aus. . .	(Yes/no,) I am from. . .
London	London
Deutschland	Germany
Ich bin Engländer	I am English (if you're a man)
Ich bin Engländerin	I am English (if you're a woman)
Ich bin auf. . .	I am on. . .
Urlaub	holiday
Geschäftsreise	business
Wo wohnen Sie?	Where do you live?
Ich wohne. . .	I live. . .
hier	here
in Ulm	in Ulm
in London	in London
Danke (schön)	Thank you (very much)
Bitte	Please
	You're welcome
Jetzt	Now

Practice what you have learned

This part of the unit is designed to help you to cope with the language you have met in the dialogues, in particular with the key phrases. You will need both the book and the cassette to do the exercises, but all the necessary instructions are in the book. Read them carefully before listening to the tape. Don't rush – there is always the pause button if things move too fast. Remember that these are *listening* exercises to help you to *understand* – your turn to speak will come later in the unit.

1 We have recorded four couples greeting each other. What time of the day is it? Listen to one couple at a time, stop the tape, tick the right box in the grid below, then go on. Rewind the tape if you haven't understood. (Answers p. 20)

		day time	morning	evening	night
a.	first couple				
b.	second couple				
c.	third couple				
d.	fourth couple				

2 Pretend you are in Germany and someone is asking you some questions about yourself. Before listening to the tape, choose the most appropriate answers for each question from the list below and write it in the space provided.

a. Wie heißen Sie? *Ich heiße Ann Smith*

b. Wo wohnen Sie? ....

c. Woher kommen Sie jetzt im Moment? ....

d. Sind Sie auf Geschäftsreise? ....

> Aus London
> Ich wohne in England
> Nein, ich bin auf Urlaub

Now turn on your cassette recorder and check if your answers are right.

3 Imagine you're on a train from Cologne to London. A fellow traveller has to fill in a form, but she has broken her arm and can't write. You offer to help her. Listen to the tape where you will hear the details, then fill in the form. (Answers p. 20)

New vocabulary
Vorname first name
Ort town

Name	....
Vorname	....
Straße	....
Ort	....

4 Peter Reynolds from Cheltenham is at an international conference in Berlin. On tape you'll hear him being introduced to four people. Which countries do they come from? Listen carefully, then complete the name tags below by filling in the appropriate country. (Answers p. 20)

New vocabulary
Spanien Spain
Italien Italy
Deutschland Germany
Österreich Austria

Herr Gonzales

Frau Husseini

Herr Velaskes

Frl. Markgraf

Grammar

You will find a grammar section in each unit, but it will be as short and simple as possible. Its aim is to give you the basics of the language so that you will have a firm ground to build on and understand how the language works. Mistakes do not matter all that much as long as you can make yourself understood.

Grammar often seems off-putting or even frightening because of its rigid patterns and abstract terms. In this course we have tried to use these as little as possible, but certain grammatical terms just cannot be avoided, e.g. 'noun', 'gender', 'article', etc. You will find a glossary of these terms on pp. 223-225.

The verb 'sein' (to be)

In Unit 1 you have come across several forms of this important verb. Here is the whole verb in its present tense. As in English, it is irregular:

ich bin	I am	**wir sind**	we are
du bist	you are	**ihr seid**	you are
er	he	**sie sind**	they are
sie ist	she is	**Sie sind**	you are
es	it		

Note the four ways of saying 'you are':

Sie sind (to one adult you don't know very well)
du bist (to one friend or child)
ihr seid (to more than one child or friend)
Sie sind (to more than one adult)

Note that there are several meanings of the word **sie**. It can mean 'she' (**sie ist Engländerin** she is English), 'they' (**wo sind sie?** where are they?), and 'you' (**wie heißen Sie?** what's your name?). Don't forget the capital for **Sie** = you!

The most important forms for you to learn at this stage are:

Sie sind. . . (or **sind Sie. . .?** in a question)
ich bin. . .
er/sie/es ist. . .

Exercise Fill in **bin, ist** or **sind** (Answers p. 20)

a. *Herr Beck:* Guten Abend.

b. *Herr Horn:* Guten Abend. .... Sie Herr Beck?

c. *Herr Beck:* Ja, ich .... Herr Beck. Und Sie?

d. *Herr Horn:* Mein Name .... Horn.

e. *Herr Beck:* .... Sie von hier?

f. *Herr Horn:* Nein, ich .... aus Berlin.

g. *Herr Beck:* Und dies .... Ihr Sohn?

h. *Herr Horn:* Ja, dies .... mein Sohn Manfred.

Read and understand

1 Here are four pictures. Study them and answer the questions below in
English. (Answers p. 20)

a. What's her husband's name? **b.** Who's being introduced?

c. What country does Mr
Martin come from?

d. Does the woman live in
Paris or in Munich?

2 Try to fill in this puzzle. You'll find the words you need all jumbled-up
below. The keyword is the name of a country. (Answers p. 20).

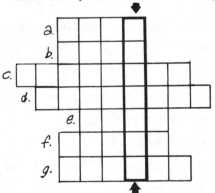

New vocabulary
sagt says
zu to

Frau
Fräulein
Name London
Portugal Sohn
Abend

a. Wie ist Ihr ....?
b. Dies ist mein Mann, und das ist mein ....
c. Eliot Fernando kommt aus ....
d. Frau oder ....?
e. Ich heiße Alfons Gräter, und meine .... heißt Anneliese
f. Cornelia Lämmermeier sagt 'Guten ....' zu Ruth
g. Cornelia kommt jetzt im Moment aus ....

Did you know?

Frau (Mrs) and Fräulein (Miss)

Officially the use of **Fräulein** has been abolished. There is, however, no equivalent of the English 'Ms', and **Frau** is the title for both married and unmarried women. In practice you will find lots of people still using **Fräulein** for unmarried and/or young women and **Frau** often for those who 'look married'. Note that when you're calling a waitress you always use **Fräulein**.

Titles

If someone has a title in Germany, he or she will usually add it to his or her name. So if you wish to flatter people (or have forgotten their names) simply address them as **Frau Professor, Herr Direktor**, etc.

First names

On the whole Germans tend to be more reserved about the use of first names than English people. If they ask you to address them by their Christian names and use **du** instead of **Sie** it usually means that you are good friends. People who work together or belong to the same kind of group often call each other **du** straight away, e.g. mountaineers, sailors, factory workers, actors. . . . And young people, especially at university or at college, seem to have abandoned the use of **Sie** altogether. But the safest rule for you would be to stick to **Sie** unless you are asked to say **du**.

Common names

Some very common surnames such as **Müller** or **Schmid (Schmidt; Schmitt)** go back to old trades and have in fact the same meaning as 'Miller' or 'Smith'. **Meyer** (and its variations **Maier, Meier, Mayer**) is another very popular name. Traditional Christian names such as **Maria** (Mary), **Hans** (John, Jack), **Josef** or **Grete** have become somewhat old-fashioned, and exotic-sounding foreign names are preferred, e.g. **Sacha, Tristan, Magnus, Mischa** (for boys), or **Tanja, Natascha, Nicole, Nathalie, Sandra** (for girls).

Your turn to speak

The exercises for this section are on your cassette. They will give you practice at saying aloud some of the most important words and phrases you have learned in a unit. For instance, you will often be asked to take part in a conversation. On the cassette our presenter Michael Wolf will give you a prompt in English. Stop the tape, then say your part aloud in German, start the tape again and listen to the correct version which will be given by either Lutz or Sabine, our two actors. You will probably need to go over the exercises a few times until you are familiar with the method used.

Each exercise is briefly introduced in your book. Read these introductions, then close your book and work with the cassette alone.

1 In the first exercise you'll be asked to take the part of Mr Müller in a conversation. You will practise
Mein Name ist . . .
Dies/das ist. . .
Meine Frau/mein Sohn/Herr Weber.

2 Stefan introduces Herr Grimm to Mrs. Arnold — you take the part of Mrs. Arnold. You'll practise
Danke, bitte
Wie ist Ihr Name?
You'll hear a new word,
Kollege – colleague.

3 This time pretend you are an Englishman from Bristol working in Munich, but living in Starnberg. You'll practise various types of questions. You'll need to know how to say
Ja, ich bin Engländer
Ich bin aus Bristol
Ja/nein
Ich wohne in Starnberg.

Answers

Practice what you have learned p. 15 Exercise 1(a) morning (b) evening (c) daytime (d) night

p. 16 Exercise 3 This is how you should have filled in the form:

Name: Mayer,
Vorname: Renate,
Straße: Hauptstraße 17,
Ort: Ulm

p. 16 Exercise 4 Herr Gonzales, **Portugal**; Frau Husseini, **Italien**; Herr Velaskes, **Österreich**; Frau Markgraf, **Deutschland**

Grammar p. 17 (b) sind (c) bin (d) ist (e) sind (f) bin (g) ist (h) ist

Read and understand p. 18 Exercise 1(a) Hermann (b) his wife (c) England (d) in Munich

p. 18 Exercise 2 (a) Name (b) Sohn (c) Portugal (d) Fräulein (e) Frau (f) Abend (g) London; keyword: **England**

2 Yourself and others

What you will learn

- to provide some basic information about yourself, your job and your family
- to say which languages you speak and that you speak a little German
- to understand and use the numbers from 1 to 20

and you will be given some background information about Germany and the German speaking countries.

Before you begin

Below you will find your study guide again. In the same way as in Unit 1, tick off the list as you go along.

Study guide

	Dialogues 1–3: listen straight through without the book
	Dialogues 1–3: listen, read and study one by one
	Dialogues 4, 5: listen straight through without the book
	Dialogues 4, 5: listen, read and study one by one
	Dialogue 6: listen several times and then study it in the book
	Dialogues 7, 8: listen straight through without the book
	Dialogues 7, 8: listen, read and study one by one and concentrate on the numbers given by the presenter
	Read and note the *Key words and phrases*
	Do the exercises in *Practice what you have learned*
	Read the *Grammar* section and do the exercises
	Do the exercises with *Read and understand*
	Read: *Did you know?*
	Do the exercises in *Your turn to speak*
	Listen to dialogues 1–8 again, this time straight through

Dialogues

1 *Ruth asks Herr Hansen about his family*

Ruth	Haben Sie Familie?
Herr Hansen	Ja, ich habe Familie, bin seit vierzehn Jahren verheiratet und habe eine Tochter.
Ruth	Und wie heißt Ihre Tochter?
Herr Hansen	Meine Tochter heißt Andrea.
Ruth	Wie alt ist sie?
Herr Hansen	Sie ist jetzt elf Jahre.

2 *Frau Reimer tells Ruth about her husband and her little daughter*

Ruth	Haben Sie Familie?
Frau Reimer	Ja. Ich habe einen Mann und eine kleine Tochter.
Ruth	Wie heißt die Tochter?
Frau Reimer	Meine Tochter heißt Julia.

3 *Is Frau Oswald married? What does she do for a living?*

Ruth	Haben Sie Familie?
Frau Oswald	Ja, ich bin verheiratet, kein Kind, bis jetzt noch.
Ruth	Und was sind Sie von Beruf?
Frau Oswald	Ich bin Angestellte am Ulmer Verkehrsbüro.

1 ♦ **haben Sie Familie?** have you got a family? Note that the 'a' is not translated.

♦ **(ich) bin seit vierzehn Jahren verheiratet** I've been married for fourteen years. When you make a statement in which past actions are still continuing, you use this construction, so 'I've been learning German for two weeks' (and I'm still learning it) is **ich lerne seit zwei Wochen Deutsch.**

♦ **ich habe eine Tochter** I have a daughter. Note that Herr Hansen leaves out the 'e' at the end of **habe: ich hab'**. This often occurs in spoken German.

♦ **Ihre/meine Tochter** your/my daughter. When speaking about a son you would say **Ihr/mein Sohn** (see Unit 1, **mein Sohn/meine Frau**).

♦ **wie alt ist sie?** how old is she?

♦ **sie ist jetzt elf Jahre** she is now eleven (years). He could also have said, **sie ist jetzt elf** or **sie ist jetzt elf Jahre alt. (das Jahr** = year)

2 ♦ **ich habe einen Mann** I have a husband.

♦ **eine kleine Tochter** a little daughter. If she had a son she would have said, **ich habe einen kleinen Sohn.** You have probably noticed the different words for the English 'a/an' in this dialogue. Don't worry about them. At this stage it is not important to understand *why* they are different. Just learn by heart that 'I have a son/husband' is **ich habe einen Sohn/Mann** – and it doesn't matter if you don't always get it right. You'll still be understood. The *important* words to learn are **Mann, Tochter,** and **Sohn.**

wie heißt die Tochter? what's your daughter called? (lit. what's the daughter called?) In German you don't have to use the equivalent of 'your' here.

3 ♦ **kein Kind** no children (lit. no child).

bis jetzt noch so far, up to now.

♦ **verheiratet** married. Other possible answers are **geschieden** (divorced), or **ledig** (single).

♦ **was sind Sie von Beruf?** what are you by profession? what's your job?

♦ **ich bin Angestellte** I am an employee. Note that you don't need the word for 'a/an' in German when you say your profession. A male employee would have said **ich bin Angestellter**. There are more examples of this in the next dialogues.

am Ulmer Verkehrsbüro at the Ulm tourist office.

4 *Ruth asks two more people about their professions*

Ruth   Was sind Sie von Beruf?
Herr Maier   Von Beruf bin ich Postbeamter.

Ruth   Was sind Sie von Beruf?
Herr Schmid   Ja, ich bin jetzt Rentner.

5 *Ruth asks Frau Reimer and Herr Schmid whether they speak other languages*

Ruth   Sprechen Sie andere Sprachen?
Frau Reimer   Ja, ich spreche etwas Englisch und Französisch.

Ruth   Sprechen Sie auch andere Sprachen?
Herr Schmid   Ah – perfekt nicht. Ich habe etwas Kenntnis in Französisch und Englisch.

auch also, as well

6(a) *At the railway station. A loudspeaker is being tested*

eins	1
zwo	2
drei	3
vier	4
fünf	5
sechs	6
sieben	7
acht	8
neun	9
zehn	10

(b) *A German counting rhyme*

**Eins, zwei, drei
du bist frei.
Vier, fünf, sechs,
du bist nächst.
Sieben, acht, neun,
du mußt's sein!**

◆ **frei** free
nächst next

4 ♦ **Postbeamter** post office official. A woman official would have said
   ♦ **Postbeamtin** (see *Grammar* section, p. 31)

   ♦ **Rentner** pensioner. A woman pensioner would have said **Rentnerin**.
   Ja means something like 'well' here.

5   **sprechen Sie andere Sprachen?** do you speak other languages?
   ♦ Note also **sprechen Sie Deutsch/Englisch/Französisch?** Do you speak
   German/English/French?

   ♦ **ja, ich spreche etwas Englisch** yes, I speak some English. Similarly:
   ♦ **ja, ich spreche etwas Französisch/Deutsch** yes, I speak some French/
   German.

   perfekt nicht not perfectly. He could also have said **nicht perfekt**.

6b   **du mußt's sein** short for **du mußt es sein** you must be it, i.e. you must be
   the one to do whatever the task is in a counting game.

   ♦ **zwei/zwo** both mean 'two'. Sometimes **zwo** is said so that you don't confuse
   the pronunciation of **zwei** and **drei**.

7 *Ruth asks Franco how long he's been in Germany*

Ruth Wie lange bist du schon in Deutschland?
Franco Vier Jahre.

8 *How long has Frau Klein been in Ulm?*

Ruth Und wie lange sind Sie schon hier?
Frau Klein Seit zehn Monaten.

7

wie lange bist du schon. . .? how long have you been. . .?
Note that the Germans use the present tense here (lit. how long are you already in Germany?)

More numbers – listen to the presenter on tape:

11 **elf**
12 **zwölf**
13 **dreizehn**
14 **vierzehn**
15 **fünfzehn**
16 **sechzehn** (Note that the 's' in sech<u>s</u> is dropped)
17 **siebzehn** (Note that the '-en' in sieb<u>en</u> is dropped)
18 **achtzehn**
19 **neunzehn**
20 **zwanzig**

8 ♦ **seit zehn Monaten** for ten months. (Remember **ich bin <u>seit</u> 14 Jahren verheiratet** in dialogue 1.) So if you're asked how long you've been in Germany you can either answer simply, as in dialogue 7, **vier Jahre** (or **zwei Wochen** two weeks, **drei Tage** three days, etc.) or as in this dialogue, e.g. <u>**seit**</u> **vier Jahren/<u>seit</u> zwei Wochen/<u>seit</u> drei Tagen** (for four years/for two weeks/for three days).
Note: after **seit** all nouns in the plural add **-n** (unless they've got an 'n' already) e.g. **der Monat** (the month), **die Monate** (months) *but* **seit vier Monate<u>n</u>** (for four months).

Key words and phrases

Haben Sie Familie?	Have you got a family?
Ja, ich habe. . .	Yes, I've got. . .
eine Frau	a wife
einen Mann	a husband
eine Tochter	a daughter
einen Sohn	a son
Nein, ich habe kein Kind	No, I haven't got any children
Ich bin. . .	I am. . .
verheiratet	married
ledig	single
geschieden	divorced
Wie alt. . .	How old. . .
ist Ihre Tochter?	is your daughter?
ist Ihr Sohn?	is your son?
Er/sie ist elf (Jahre alt)	He/she is eleven (years old)
Und was sind Sie von Beruf?	And what's your job?
Ich bin. . .	I am. . .
Rentner(in)	a pensioner
Angestellte(r)	an employee, a clerk
Postbeamter/Postbeamtin	a post office official
Wie lange. . .	How long. . .
sind Sie schon in Ulm?	have you been in Ulm?
arbeiten Sie schon (am	have you been working (at the
Verkehrsbüro)?	tourist office)?
Drei Jahre	Three years
Vier Wochen	Four weeks
Seit. . .	For. . .
vierzehn Monaten	fourteen months
zwölf Jahren	twelve years
Sprechen Sie. . .	Do you speak. . .
Englisch?	English?
Französisch?	French?
Deutsch?	German?
Ja, ich spreche (etwas). . .	Yes, I speak (a little). . .
Englisch	English
Französisch	French
Deutsch	German

Numbers 1 – 20 are written out in the notes for dialogues 6 and 7.

Practice what you have learned

Now we're coming to the listening section again where you'll have a chance to practice the most important words and phrases you've already heard in the dialogues. Again your chance to speak will come later in this unit. Read the instructions for each exercise before you listen to the tape.

1 Listen to the tape where you will hear a hotel porter telling you the room numbers of some people. Fill in their room numbers in the boxes below. (Answers p. 34)

New vocabulary: **Zimmer-Nummer** room number

Zimmer-Nummer

a.	Frau Müller	
b.	Herr Schmitt	
c.	Frl. Wolf	
d.	Frau Haller	
e.	Herr Dron	

2 Listen to the tape. Four people are dialling telephone numbers. Whose numbers are they dialling? Tick them off on the list below. (Answers p. 34)

☐	Abel 33857
☐	Dron 11697
☐	Gross 12345
☐	Haller 73783
☐	Müller 33957
☐	Otto 22758
☐	Schmitt 22857
☐	Wolf 12369

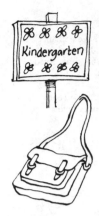

3 Ruth is asking two little boys some questions. Listen to the dialogue, then decide whether the statements below are True or False (**Richtig oder Falsch**) and tick the right box. (Answers p. 34)

New vocabulary: **Schule** school

a. Ruth asks the boys where they live R   F

b. The boys are called Thomas and Robert R   F

c. Thomas is seven years old R   F

d. Robert is younger than Thomas R   F

e. They both go to school R   F

4 For this exercise, write the answers *before* you listen to the tape. Select the correct sentences from the box below to complete the dialogue and write them in the spaces. Then listen to the tape to see whether they fit.

Sprechen Sie Deutsch? ....

....

Wie lange sind Sie schon hier? ....

....

Haben Sie Familie? ....

....

Wie alt ist Ihr Sohn? ....

....

Er ist jetzt zwei Monate alt.

Seit vier Wochen.

Ja, ich spreche etwas Deutsch!

Ich habe einen Mann und einen kleinen Sohn.

Grammar

The verb 'haben' (to have)

Haben and **sein** (to be) are two of the most important verbs. They are both irregular, but not difficult to memorize. Pay special attention to the **ich** and **Sie** forms which are the ones you will probably need most. Below are all the forms of **haben** in the present tense.

ich habe	I have	**wir haben**	we have
du hast	you have	**ihr habt**	you have
er ⎫	he ⎫	**sie haben**	they have
sie ⎬ **hat**	she ⎬ has	**Sie haben**	you have (polite form)
es ⎭	it ⎭		

Exercise 1 Fill in the right forms of **haben**. (Answers p. 34)

a. H............ Sie Familie? **c.** H............ Frau Meier eine Tochter?

b. Ja, ich h............ einen Sohn. **d.** Nein, Frau Meier h............ kein Kind.

Regular verbs

Luckily not all verbs are irregular in German. The basic pattern for all verbs is as follows. We'll use **wohnen** (to live) as an example.

ich wohne	I live	**wir wohnen**	we live
du wohnst	you live	**ihr wohnt**	you live
er ⎫	he ⎫	**sie wohnen**	they live
sie ⎬ **wohnt**	she ⎬ lives	**Sie wohnen**	you live (polite form)
es ⎭	it ⎭		

So the rule is that you add the endings (underlined above) to the stem (**wohn-**), which is the main part of the verb. There are some small exceptions to this rule but these are mostly because of awkward spelling or pronunciation. For example,

heißen (to be called) **ich heiße, du heißt, er (sie, es) heißt, wir heißen, ihr heißt, sie (Sie) heißen.** ß is the symbol which is the equivalent of **ss**, so there is no need for an extra 's' in **du heißt**.

Exercise 2 Write out the present tense of the verb **kommen** (to come), with the translations, in the same way as we have written the verb **wohnen** in this section. (Answers p. 34)

More on nouns

In German the ending of a word denoting a profession quite often changes according to sex, just as in English you have waiter/waitress. A male pensioner is **ein Rentner**, a female pensioner is **eine Rentnerin**. Here are some more examples:

ein Student, eine Studentin (a student)
ein Sekretär, eine Sekretärin (a secretary)
ein Verkäufer, eine Verkäuferin (a shop assistant)
ein Arbeiter, eine Arbeiterin (a worker)
ein Direktor, eine Direktorin (a director)
ein Schüler, eine Schülerin (a pupil)

But: ein Angestellter, eine Angestellte (an employee).

Read and understand

Read the following passage and answer the questions below in English.
(Answers p. 34)

1 Frau Müller ist verheiratet. Sie hat eine kleine Tochter und drei Söhne.
Die Tochter ist fünf, und die Söhne sind neun, zwölf und vierzehn Jahre
alt. Ihr Mann ist Postbeamter und arbeitet in Bonn. Sie sind seit sechzehn
Jahren verheiratet und wohnen seit zwei Jahren in Bonn.

a. Is Frau Müller divorced? ....

b. Does she have three daughters? ....

c. How old are her sons? ....

d. Where do they live? ....

e. What does her husband do? ....

f. How long have they been married? ....

2 Look at the pictures, read the words and tick the right box.
(Answers p. 34)

a. Fritz ist

☐ Schüler

☐ Rentner

☐ Angestellte

b. Viktoria ist

☐ Direktor

☐ Postbeamter

☐ Studentin

c. Herr Kinder ist

☐ Beamtin

☐ Sekretär

☐ Verkäuferin

d. Frau Schmitt ist

☐ Angestellter

☐ Verkäuferin

☐ Beamter

Did you know?

German is the official language of the Federal Republic of Germany, the German Democratic Republic (GDR), Austria, Switzerland (together with French, Italian and Romanic), and the Principality of **Liechtenstein**. Some German is also spoken in the **Elsaß** region (Alsace, in France) and in **Südtirol** (South Tyrol, a region in Northern Italy).

The Federal Republic is the largest of the German-speaking countries with an area of 375,000 square kilometres and a population of 79 million (UK 244,000 square kilometeres, 56 million inhabitants).

The Federal Republic is called 'Federal' because it consists of a federation of sixteen **Länder** (states). **Bayern** is the largest in area, but **Nordrhein-Westfalen** (Northrhine-Westfalia) is the most populous. The **Ruhrgebiet** (an area east of Düsseldorf along the river **Ruhr)** is the largest single industrial region in Europe, producing a third of Germany's exports (mainly machinery).

There are several million foreigners living in the Federal Republic. Most of them are **Gastarbeiter** (immigrant workers, lit. 'guest workers') from Turkey, Italy, Spain, Yugoslavia and Greece and more recently from Eastern Europe.

The Federal Republic has borders with nine countries — Poland, Czechoslovakia, Austria, Switzerland, France, Belgium, Luxemburg, the Netherlands, and Denmark.

Your turn to speak

1   On the cassette you'll be asked to take part in a dialogue again. You'll be prompted in English. Say your part in German.
You'll be practicing,

Ich bin . . .
Ich habe . . .
Mark/Angela ist . . .

2   This time *you* must ask the questions. Imagine you're in Ulm and you've just been introduced to Angelika and want to find out a bit more about her. You'll practice:

Sind Sie . . .?
Wo . . .?
Sprechen Sie . . .?

Answers

Practice what you have learned p. 29 Exercise 1(a) 3 (b) 2 (c) 7 (d) 9 (e) 4

p. 29 Exercise 2 You should have ticked the numbers of **Wolf, Haller, Schmitt,** and **Müller.**

p. 30 Exercise 3 (a) F (b) R (c) F (d) R (e) F

Grammar p. 31 Exercise 1(a) Haben (b) habe (c) hat (d) hat

p. 31 Exercise 2

ich komme	I come	wir kommen	we come
du kommst	you come	ihr kommt	you come
er ⎫	he ⎫	sie kommen	they come
sie ⎬ kommt	she ⎬ comes	Sie kommen	you come
es ⎭	it ⎭		

Read and understand p. 32 Exercise 1(a) no, she's married (b) no, she's got three sons and one daughter (c) nine, twelve and fourteen (d) in Bonn (e) a post office official (f) for 16 years

p. 32 Exercise 2(a) Schüler (b) Studentin (c) Sekretär (e) Verkäuferin

3 Getting information

What you will learn

- to ask for a room at a hotel
- to ask how much it is and whether it includes breakfast
- to ask the way to your room, the bank, etc.
- to understand the basic answers to all these questions
- what to say when you want to change money
- numbers from 20 onwards

and you will learn where and when to change money, and be given some general guidelines on different types of accommodation in Germany.

Study guide

	Dialogues 1–3: listen through without book
	Dialogues 1–3: listen, read and study one by one
	Dialogues 4, 5: listen only
	Dialogues 4, 5: listen and read the notes
	Dialogues 6–8: listen without book
	Dialogues 6–8: listen and read the notes
	Study the *Key words and phrases*
	Do the exercises in *Practice what you have learned*
	Study the *Grammar* section closely
	Do the exercises in *Read and understand*
	Read: *Did you know?*
	Do *Your turn to speak*
	Listen to all the dialogues again straight through

Dialogues

1 *At the reception of the Münster hotel*

Ruth	Grüß Gott.
Frau Pichler	Grüß Gott. Was wünschen Sie?
Ruth	Haben Sie noch ein Zimmer frei?
Frau Pichler	Ja . . . ein Doppelzimmer oder Einzelzimmer?
Ruth	Ein Einzelzimmer bitte.

‣ **das Doppelzimmer** the double room
‣ **das Einzelzimmer** the single room

(For an explanation of **das**, and **der/die** see *Grammar* section p. 45)

2 *How much is the room?*

Ruth	Und was würde das kosten?
Frau Pichler	Das kostet vierzig Mark, das Einzelzimmer mit Dusche. Und ein Einzelzimmer ohne Dusche dreißig Mark.
Ruth	Ein Einzelzimmer mit Dusche, bitte.
Frau Pichler	Mit Dusche . . . kostet dann vierzig Mark, inklusiv Frühstück.

dann then

3 *How long would Ruth like to stay?*

Frau Pichler	Wie lange? Für eine Nacht, oder möchten Sie eine Woche bleiben?
Ruth	Ja, ich möchte gerne vier Tage bleiben.
Frau Pichler	Können Sie. Das kostet dann pro Nacht vierzig Mark.
Ruth	Gut.

pro Nacht per night

A hotel reception desk

1   was wünschen Sie? what would you like?

♦ haben Sie noch ein Zimmer frei? have you still got a room (free)?

2   was würde das kosten? what would that cost? You don't have to learn the use of würde yet. As with the English 'would,' it is used when you want to
♦ be more polite, but you can just ask was kostet das? (how much is it?); kosten = to cost.

♦ mit/ohne Dusche with/without a shower. You might also be asked mit oder ohne Balkon/Bad/WC? (with or without a balcony/bath/WC?) Note that again the 'a' is not translated – the Germans simply say mit Dusche (with shower).

inklusiv Frühstück including breakfast. You may want to ask,
♦ ist Frühstück inklusiv? is breakfast included?

Note that prices vary widely. Depending on where you are, you may have to spend two or three times as much.

3   wie lange? für eine Nacht? how long? for one night?

oder möchten Sie eine Woche bleiben? or would you like to stay a week?

♦ ich möchte gerne vier Tage bleiben I'd very much like to stay four days.
ich möchte (I'd like) is a very useful phrase, so make sure you've really learned it, and note the word order in any sentence using
möchte, e.g.
ich möchte eine Woche *bleiben* I'd like to stay a week
ich möchte in München *wohnen* I'd like to live in Munich
ich möchte in London *arbeiten* I'd like to work in London.
You'll notice that in German the second verb in a sentence, e.g. bleiben, wohnen, arbeiten, goes to the *end.*

♦ ich möchte gerne I'd very much like (lit. I'd like willingly);
gerne (or gern) is often used with ich möchte if you want to be even more polite or if you want to add emphasis, e.g. ich möchte gerne ein Zimmer mit Dusche, ich möchte gern in London bleiben.

können Sie you can. The receptionist is simply affirming 'you can stay'. She could as well have said Sie können.

4 *At the Bundesbahn hotel, where Ruth has reserved a double room*

Ruth	Guten Tag.
Fräulein Lind	Guten Tag.
Ruth	Ich habe bei Ihnen ein Zimmer reserviert.
Fräulein Lind	Ein Doppel – oder ein Einzelzimmer?
Ruth	Ein Doppelzimmer, und der Name ist Rach.
Fräulein Lind	Ja, kleinen Moment bitte . . . So. Das wäre Zimmer 115 für Sie, auf dem ersten Stock. Wie lange bleiben Sie bitte?
Ruth	Ich bleibe eine Woche.

5 *Ruth gets her key and asks about breakfast*

Fräulein Lind	So bitte. Hier ist Ihr Schlüssel.
Ruth	Danke schön.
Fräulein Lind	Erste Etage.
Ruth	Bitte?
Fräulein Lind	Erste Etage!
Ruth	Und – eh – wann ist Frühstück?
Fräulein Lind	Frühstück ist von sechs Uhr bis zehn Uhr dreißig.
Ruth	Im Parterre?
Fräulein Lind	Ja.
Ruth	Danke schön.
Fräulein Lind	Bitte sehr.

♦ **der Schlüssel** key

6 *Ruth asks Frau Oswald at the tourist office where the nearest bank is*

Ruth	Wo ist die nächste Bank bitte?
Frau Oswald	Die nächste Bank? Die liegt gleich zwanzig Meter vom Verkehrsbüro, also direkt im Zentrum am Münsterplatz.

direkt directly

4   **ich habe (bei Ihnen) ein Zimmer reserviert** I have reserved a room (with you).

kleinen Moment just a moment.

das wäre . . . that would be. Or she could simply have said,
das ist Zimmer 115.

für Sie for you.

auf dem ersten Stock on the first floor.

5   **erste Etage** first floor. There is no real difference in the use of **Stock** (see dialogue 4) and **Etage**, both are common.

‣ **bitte?** means here 'I beg your pardon?'

‣ **wann ist Frühstück?** when is breakfast?

‣ **von sechs Uhr bis zehn Uhr dreißig** from six o'clock to ten thirty. (More about time in Unit 6.)

im Parterre on the ground floor.

bitte sehr you're very welcome, it's a pleasure – even more polite than just **bitte.**

6 ‣ **wo ist die nächste Bank bitte?** where is the nearest bank please?

die nächste Bank? Die liegt gleich zwanzig Meter vom Verkehrsbüro the nearest bank? That's just 20 metres from the tourist office. If you refer back to something mentioned previously you simply say **der, die,** or **das** (lit. the) and leave out the noun, e.g. **Die Bank? Die liegt im Zentrum.** The bank? That's in the centre. **Der Schlüssel? Der ist hier.** The key? That's here. **Das Zimmer? Das ist noch frei.** The room? That's still free. (**der, die,** and **das** are dealt with thoroughly in the *Grammar* section, p. 45).

am Münsterplatz on/by Münster square.

7 Changing money at the bank

Ruth Guten Tag.
Frau Kolb Guten Tag.
Ruth Ich möchte gerne fünfzig Pfund umwechseln, bitte.
Frau Kolb Ein Pfund sind vier Mark und vier, dann sind das – Moment – zweihundertundzwei Mark.
Ruth Ja, gut.
Frau Kolb Dann kommen Sie bitte an die Kasse.

  ◗ **umwechseln** (or **wechseln**) to change

8 At the teller's window

Frau Kolb Wie möchten Sie's?
Ruth In kleinen Scheinen bitte.
Frau Kolb Fünfzig (50), einhundert (100), fünfzig, zwohundert (200), zwohundertzwo (202). Bitte sehr!
Ruth Danke schön.
Frau Kolb Danke auch. Auf Wiedersehen!

  ◗ **auf Wiedersehen** good-bye

7 ♦ **fünfzig Pfund** fifty pounds. The numbers from 20 onwards will appear in *Key words and phrases*, p. 42.

♦ **vier Mark und vier** four marks and four. At the time, Ruth got four marks and four pennies (**Pfennige**) for one British pound, but the exchange rate may well be different now. One **Deutsche Mark** (DM) has 100 **Pfennige**, and there are one, two, five, ten and fifty **Pfennig** pieces, one, two, and five **Mark** coins, and ten, twenty, fifty, one hundred, five hundred, and one thousand **Mark** notes.

kommen Sie bitte an die Kasse please come to the teller's window. Note the word order in a request, e.g. **kommen Sie bitte** (lit. come you please). Similarly: **gehen Sie bitte** (please go), **sprechen Sie bitte** (please speak).

8 **wie möchten Sie's?** short for **wie möchten Sie es?** how would you like it?

in kleinen Scheinen in small notes.

50,100 . . . Frau Kolb is handing out the money in fifty **Mark** notes.

bitte sehr in this case means 'here you are'.

danke auch short for **ich danke auch** I thank you too.

Key words and phrases

Haben Sie noch ein Zimmer frei?	Have you still got a room (free)?
Ich habe ein Zimmer reserviert	I have reserved a room
Ein Einzelzimmer/Doppelzimmer mit . . .	A single/double room with . . .
Bad	bath
Dusche	shower
Balkon	balcony
WC . . ., bitte	WC . . ., please

Ich möchte (gerne) . . .	I'd (very much) like to . . .
eine Woche bleiben	stay a week
vier Tage bleiben	stay four days
20 Pfund wechseln	change 20 pounds

Ist Frühstück inklusiv?	Is breakfast included?
Wann ist Frühstück?	When's breakfast?

Wo ist . . .	Where is . . .
der Schlüssel?	the key?
das Bad?	the bathroom?
das WC?	the WC?
die nächste Bank?	the nearest bank?

Was kostet das?	How much is it?
Auf Wiedersehen	Good-bye

Numbers from 20 onwards

20	zwanzig
30	dreißig
40	vierzig
50	fünfzig
60	sechzig
70	siebzig
80	achtzig
90	neunzig
100	(ein) hundert
200	zweihundert
300	dreihundert
400	vierhundert
500	fünfhundert
600	sechshundert
700	siebenhundert
800	achthundert
900	neunhundert
1000	(ein) tausend
2000	zweitausend
10,000	zehntausend
100,000	hunderttausend
1,000,000	eine Million

$21 = 1 + 20$ einundzwanzig
$22 = 2 + 20$ zweiundzwanzig
$101 =$ einhundertundeins
$634 =$ sechshundertvierunddreißig

Practice what you have learned

1 On the tape you will hear two dialogues of people booking hotel rooms. What kind of room are they booking? Listen carefully and tick or fill in the right boxes in the grid below. (Answers p. 48)

		a.	b.
⊢━┤	Einzelzimmer		
⊢━┥	Doppelzimmer		
(shower)	Dusche		
(bath)	Bad		
[WC]	WC		
☎	Telefon		
	Das kostet pro Nacht DM		
	Wie lange? (Tage)		
	Das kostet zusammen DM		
	Zimmer-Nr.		

2 This time you will hear two people in a bank wanting to change money. Listen carefully to find out how much they want to change, what the exchange rate was then and how many DM they get in return. Then fill in the grid below. (Answers p. 48)

	Dollar	Franc
Wieviel? (how much?)		
Kurs? (exchange rate?)		
Wieviel DM sind das?		

3 The hotel manager asks his secretary to get the invoices ready for the guests who are leaving. He reads the room numbers and the sums of money out to her. Listen to him on your cassette, then write down the room numbers and the respective amounts of DM. (Answers p. 48)

	Zimmer-Nr.	DM
a.	18	73,80
b.		
c.		
d.		
e.		
f.		

A modern 'Holiday Inn' in Frankfurt (behind an old 'Lookout Tower')

Grammar

German nouns

All nouns in German are written with a capital initial letter, e.g. **die Frau** (the woman).

There are three categories of nouns, called *genders* – masculine, feminine, and neuter. You can tell the gender of a noun by the words for 'the' and 'a'.

masculine	**der Mann**	the man	**ein Mann**	a man
feminine	**die Frau**	the woman	**eine Frau**	a woman
neuter	**das Kind**	the child	**ein Kind**	a child

Sometimes the gender is obvious, e.g. **der Vater** (the father) is masculine, and **die Mutter** (the mother) feminine. But unfortunately in most cases the gender is arbitrary. It is for instance <u>das</u> **Fräulein** and who would have thought of a **Fräulein** as a neuter! Note the gender of the following: **die Bank, die Dusche, das Zimmer, das Hotel, der Tag, der Morgen, die Nacht,** etc. There are very few rules to help; the gender of the noun just has to be learnt. When we introduce new vocabulary from now on, we will always include **der, die,** or **das** with a noun so that you know its gender. (In the vocabulary list at the back of the book they will be shown as **m., f.,** or **n.**). Try and learn the genders of nouns as well as you can, but don't get too worried if you get them wrong – you'll still be understood.

Unfortunately you will find that learning **der, die, das** and **ein, eine, ein** is not the end of the story. Study the following sentences:

der/ein Schlüssel ist hier   the/a key is here
ich habe den/einen Schlüssel   I've got the/a key

Note that in the second sentence **der** changes to **de<u>n</u>** and **ein** to **ein<u>en</u>**. This occurs when a masculine noun is the *direct object* in a sentence. (For definition of *object* see p. 224). No change occurs when feminine and neuter nouns become direct objects, e.g.

die/eine Uhr ist hier   the/a watch is here
ich habe die/eine Uhr   I've got the/a watch

das/ein Zimmer ist hier   the/a room is here

ich habe das/ein Zimmer   I've got the/a room

When a noun becomes a direct object, grammar books would call this the *accusative case*. There are four cases altogether in German. At this stage, just be aware that these cases involve changes in certain words (particularly 'the' and 'a' and nouns and adjectives) and we'll deal with them as they come up. You'll find a complete list for your reference at the back of the book on p. 224.

Read and understand

1 Study this letterhead and read the following statements. Are they True or False? (**Richtig oder Falsch?**) (Answers p. 48)

New vocabulary
fließend warm und kalt Wasser hot and cold running water
der Parkplatz parking lot

Münster Hotel
Hotel garni am Münster
7900 Ulm-Donau
Münsterplatz 14
Telefon (0731) 64162)

Direkt am Münster
Moderne Zimmer
Fließend warm und kalt Wasser
Parkplatz

a. Das Hotel ist in München ☐R ☐F

b. Es hat eine Sauna ☐R ☐F

c. Es hat einen Parkplatz ☐R ☐F

d. Die Zimmer sind alt ☐R ☐F

e. Es ist am Münsterplatz ☐R ☐F

2 Read what kind of hotel room the following people would like and then see what the various hotels and boarding houses below have to offer. Where would each person be most happy? Write their names under the hotels. (Answers p. 48)

 Gisela Schmidt: Ich möchte ein Einzelzimmer mit Bad und Telefon

 Volker Nagel: Ich möchte ein Doppelzimmer mit Bad und WC, Telefon und TV

 Hanna Moser: ein Einzelzimmer mit fließend warm and kalt Wasser

 Gerd Hanke: ein Zimmer in einem Hotel mit Hausbar und Sauna

a. *Hotel Sonnenhof*

b. *Pension König*

....

....

c. *Hotel Europa*

d. *Gasthof Bavaria*

....

....

Did you know?

HOTELS IN
DEUTSCHEN STÄDTEN

Where to stay

A wide range of accommodation is available in Germany to suit most tastes and budgets. First there are of course hotels. Standards and prices vary enormously, but generally hotels are cheaper in rural areas and in the outskirts of cities. The local tourist office will usually be able to refer you to a hotel of your specification, or there will be a list of rooms with prices and telephone numbers on display outside the tourist office. At airports and large railway stations there is usually a counter with a sign **Zimmernachweis** (accommodation register) where you can book a room. If in doubt about standards and prices, look at the Michelin Guide or a similar guide.

Inns, pensions, holiday houses

Rooms in a **Pension** (*pension*, boarding house), a **Garni** (bed and breakfast), or a **Gasthoff** (inn) tend to be cheaper than hotels, but again standards and prices vary considerably. Many of the country inns still have their own butcher, and the food is often excellent. You'll also often find accommodation available in private houses, especially in holiday areas. Enquire at the local tourist office, or look for signs **Zimmer frei** (rooms available). But keep in mind that breakfast is usually not included in the price — if it is served at all. A **Ferienwohnung** (holiday apartment) or **Ferienhaus** (holiday house) might suit you better — they are self-contained and you can do your own cooking. **Ferien auf dem Bauernhof** (farm holidays) are good value and great fun, especially for children. They are becoming more and more popular, so book well in advance. Details are available from the German Tourist Office in New York, the regional tourist offices in Germany (**Verkehrsbüros**), or, if you can, read the advertisements in German papers like *Süddeutsche Zeitung* or *Die Zeit*.

Camping sites, youth hostels and similar accommodation

Campingplätze (camping sites) are all over Germany; they tend to become rather crowded in the summer. The **ADAC** (German Automobile Association) issues a guidebook for campers. **Jugendherbergen** (youth hostels) may be used by all young people under 24. In addition adults over 24 may stay there, too, – except in Bavaria – if there are still beds vacant after 7 p.m. In the peak season it is advisable to book in advance. To get a bed you need an International Youth Hostel Association membership card. YMCA hostels exist in many large towns; they are also mainly for young people. **Naturfreundehäuser** (Friends of Nature hostels) are located in scenically attractive regions. Some are hiking centres, or youth guest houses, but it is also possible for others to stay overnight if they book. In the Bavarian, Swiss and Austrian Alps you will find that a **Berghütte** (mountain hut) will put you up if you're hiking or mountaineering – if they can fit you in.

Where to change money

Many hotel receptions will change your money for you. You will also find **Geldwechsel** (exchange) at all major railway stations and at airports. They tend to have longer opening hours than the banks, but their rates could be slightly higher.

Banks are open Mondays to Fridays from 9 to 12.30 and from 2 to 4.00. Slight variations are possible from region to region.

You will find a list of useful addresses on p. 239.

Your turn to speak

Have another look at the *Key phrases* on p. 42. Here you'll have a chance to practice speaking some of them. Listen to the tape. Michael will tell you what to say as usual.

1   You are getting yourself a room in a hotel. You'll practise:

Haben Sie ein Zimmer frei?
Ein Einzelzimmer
Was kostet . . .
. . . mit Dusche

2   You want to change money. You'll practice:

Wo ist . . .
Ich möchte gerne . . .

Revision/Review

Now a chance to go over again some of the important language you have learned in Units 1–3. Turn to the back of your book p. 217 for what to do. You will also need your tape recorder.

Answers

Practice what you have learned p. 43 Exercise **1** (**a**) woman: **Doppelzimmer**; **Dusche**; Das kostet pro Nacht DM 50, Wie lange? 2 Tage; Das kostet zusammen DM 100; Zimmer-Nr. **14** (**b**) man: **Doppelzimmer, Bad, WC, Telefon**; Das kostet pro Nacht DM **80**, Wie lange? **10** Tage; Das kostet zusammen DM **800**; Zimmer-Nr. 24

p. 43 Exercise **2** Dollar: **150** (Wieviel?); **1 Dollar = 2,10 DM** (Kurs); **315** (Wieviel DM sind das?); Franc: **500** (Wieviel?) **100 F = 43,30 DM** (Kurs); **216,50 DM** (Wieviel DM sind das?)
p. 44 Exercise **3**(**b**) 25, DM 112,50 (**c**) 37, DM 334,70 (**d**) 39, DM 58, (**e**) 41, DM 630,90 (**f**) 50, DM 710,10

Read and understand p. 46 Exercise **1**(**a**) F (**b**) F (**c**) R (**d**) F (**e**) R
p. 46 Exercise **2**(**a**) Gisela Schmidt (**b**) Hanna Moser (**c**) Gerd Hanke (**d**) Volker Nagel

4 Ordering drinks and snacks

What you will learn

- to order breakfast
- to ask for a seat at a table
- to order drinks, snacks and desserts
- to ask for the bill
  and you will be given some information about breakfast habits and where to buy snacks.

Study guide

	Dialogues 1, 2: listen without the book
	Dialogues 1, 2: listen, read and study one by one
	Dialogues 3–5: listen without the book
	Dialogues 3–5: listen, read and study one by one
	Dialogues 6, 7: listen several times
	Dialogues 6, 7: listen, read and study one by one
	Study *Key words and phrases*
	Read *Did you know?* (*before* listening exercises!)
	Do *Practice what you have learned*
	Study the *Grammar* section and do the exercise
	Do the exercises in *Read and understand*
	Do the exercises in *Your turn to speak*
	Listen to all the dialogues again straight through

Dialogues

1 *Ruth orders breakfast*

Frau Pichler	Guten Morgen. Was wünschen Sie? Tee, Kaffee, Kakao, heiße Milch, kalte Milch, dazu ein weiches Ei?
Ruth	Ich möchte gerne ein Kännchen Tee, bitte.
Frau Pichler	Mit Zitrone oder mit Milch?
Ruth	Mit Zitrone bitte.
Frau Pichler	Danke schön.

- **der Tee** tea
- **der Kaffee** coffee
- **der Kakao** cocoa
- **die Zitrone** lemon

2 *Ruth buys some rolls*

Ruth	Grüß Gott.
Verkäuferin	Grüß Gott. Was darf's sein?
Ruth	Fünf Brötchen bitte.
Verkäuferin	Jawohl. Eine Mark fünfundneunzig bitte. Danke! . . . Bitte schön.
Ruth	Danke schön.

1 ◆ **heiße Milch, kalte Milch?** hot milk, cold milk? Words like **heiß** (hot) and **kalt** (cold) are adjectives (see Glossary p. 225 for definition). Their endings change according to the gender of the following noun. **Milch** is feminine (**die Milch**), so **heiß** and **kalt** add **-e**. Remember **meine Frau** from Unit 1 – that's the same principle. You'll find more about adjective endings in Unit 7, and you'll find a list of adjective endings on p. 225.

◆ **dazu ein weiches Ei?** a soft-boiled egg with it? Here we have a neuter noun – **das Ei**. In this case the adjective **weich** (soft, soft-boiled) adds **-es**.

◆ **ein Kännchen Tee** a small pot of tea. A word which ends in **-chen** means that the object is small, e.g. **die Kanne** – the pot, **das Kännchen** – the small pot, **das Haus** – the house, **das Häuschen** – the small house. Words ending in **-chen** are *always* neuter. A similar ending is **-lein** – remember **das Fräulein** – 'little woman'.

Here are some more items you might want to order for breakfast: **der Orangensaft** (orange juice), **der Grapefruitsaft** (grapefruit juice), **der Apfelsaft** (apple juice), **der Tomatensaft** (tomato juice), **der Toast** (toast), **die Marmelade** (jam; marmalade), **der Käse** (cheese), **die Wurst** (sausage), **das Brot** (bread), **die Butter** (butter), **der Zucker** (sugar). **Der/die/das** are given for reference only. If you wanted to order for example 'some toast, marmalade and butter' you'd simply say, **ich möchte gerne Toast, Marmelade und Butter.**

2 ◆ **was darf's sein?** short for **was darf es sein?** can I help you? (lit. what may it be?)

◆ **das Brötchen** the roll. Another word ending in **-chen** (lit. 'little bread', from **Brot** = bread)

jawohl a stronger, more affirmative way of saying 'yes'.

bitte schön here you are. The shop assistant says this as she hands Ruth her change. She could also have said **bitte sehr**; there is no difference.

☐ **3** *Ruth's friend Renate is looking for a seat in a pub*

Renate Guten Tag. Ist hier noch frei?
Frau Nein, hier ist leider besetzt.

☐ **4** *In the pub. Renate orders a drink*

Fräulein Grüß Gott. Sie wünschen bitte?
Renate Ein Bier bitte.
Fräulein Ein großes oder ein kleines?
Renate Ein kleines.
Fräulein Möchten Sie auch die Speisekarte?
Rente Ja bitte, gerne.
Fräulein Hmm.

♦ **das Bier** beer
♦ **die Speisekarte** (or **die Karte**) menu

☐ **5** *The choice of snacks*

Renate Und was haben Sie auf der kalten Karte?
Fräulein Oh, da haben wir verschiedene Wurstsalate, Ochsenmaulsalat, russische Eier, belegte Brote mit Schinken, Salami, und so weiter, und Rippchen. . . .

verschieden various
der Schinken ham
die Salami salami
und so weiter etcetera (lit. and so forth)
das Rippchen sparerib

KALTE GERICHTE

Wurstbrot (6) .... DM 2,50
Käsebrot .... DM 2,80
Salamibrot .... DM 3,30
Lachsbrot mit Zwiebelringen (1,2,3,5) .... DM 3,50
Schinkenbrot .... DM 3,90

Ochsenmaulsalat mit Brot (3,4) .... DM 3,80
Wurstsalat mit Brot (6) .... DM 4,--
Wurstsalat "Schweizer Art" mit Brot (6) .... DM 4,50
Russische Eier mit Brot (1,2,6) .... DM 5,50
Ripple mit Brot .... DM 5,80

3 ♦ **ist hier noch frei?** is this (seat) still vacant?

leider unfortunately.

♦ **besetzt** taken; occupied.

4 ♦ **ein großes oder ein kleines?** a large or a small (one)?
Again the adjectives **groß** (large) and **klein** (small) have to add **-es** because **Bier** is a neuter noun: **das Bier.** A large beer is usually ½ litre and a small one ⅓ litre (1 litre = 1.76 pints).

♦ To order some wine Renate would have said **ein Glas Wein bitte** (a glass of wine, please). There is **Rotwein** (red wine) and **Weißwein** (white wine).

möchten Sie auch die Speisekarte? would you also like the menu? Or she
♦ could have said, **möchten Sie auch etwas zu essen?** would you like something to eat?

ja bitte, gerne yes, please. **Gerne** is added to be more polite.

You might like to know some of the many words for 'pub': **die Gaststätte, der Gasthof, die Wirtschaft, das Lokal, die Kneipe** (colloquial), **die Pinte** (colloquial), **die Beitz** (colloquial in South Germany and Switzerland).

5 ♦ **auf der kalten Karte** on the snack menu. On this type of menu you'll find cold dishes which can be ordered all through the day.

verschiedene Wurstsalate various sausage salads. A 'sausage salad' is quite different from for example an English ham salad. It consists of thinly cut pieces of sausage or cold meat and onions, served with a French dressing.

(der) Ochsenmaulsalat (lit. ox muzzle salad) – a South German speciality.

russische Eier eggs in mayonnaise (lit. Russian eggs).

♦ **belegte Brote** slices of bread topped with sausage, cold meat, cheese or smoked fish. **Brote** is the plural of **das Brot** (bread) – see *Grammar* section p. 59. Instead of **belegte Brote** you will sometimes find 'sandwiches' written up instead.

Gold Ochsen
Die große Ulmer
Traditions-Brauerei

6 *Ordering a piece of cake and some coffee for dessert*

Renate Haben Sie auch Kuchen?
Fräulein Ja, zur Zeit haben wir Erdbeertorte aus frischen Erdbeeren und
Käsesahnetorte, mit oder oder Sahne.
Renate Dann nehme ich ein Kännchen Kaffee, und eine Erdbeertorte.
Fräulein Mit Sahne?
Renate Ohne Sahne bitte.
Fräulein Ohne Sahne. Sie sind für die schlanke Linie.

♦ **der Kuchen** cake
♦ **die Sahne** (whipped) cream
  zur Zeit at the moment

7 *And now the bill*

Renate Bezahlen bitte!
Fräulein Ja, elf Mark vierzig bitte.

6

> die **Erdbeertorte** strawberry cake. **Die Erdbeere** = strawberry,
>   **die Torte** = cake, flan.

aus **frischen Erdbeeren** (made) with fresh strawberries.

die **Käsesahnetorte** a rich cheesecake.

Sie sind für die schlanke Linie you're thinking of your figure (**schlanke Linie** = slimline).

> **dann nehme ich** . . . in that case I'll take . . . (lit. then take I . . .) The word order in a sentence is normally like this: **ich nehme dann ein Kännchen Kaffee** (I take (then) a pot of coffee), i.e. it starts with the subject, **ich** (I). If you don't want to start with the subject but with e.g. **dann** (then), the subject and verb change places – **dann nehme ich.** There's another example in this dialogue: **zur Zeit haben wir Erdbeertorte** (at the moment we have (lit. have we) strawberry cake). The main verb in the sentence is then usually in second place.

More useful vocabulary for ordering desserts or drinks:
> ein **Stück Kuchen/Torte** a piece of cake
> eine **Tasse Kaffee/Tee** a cup of coffee/tea
> ein **Glas Bier/Saft/Wein** a glass of beer/juice/wine
> der **Nachtisch** dessert.

7

> **bezahlen bitte** the bill please. **Bezahlen** (or simply **zahlen**) = to pay. As you know from Unit 1, 'waitress' is **Fräulein.** You would call a waiter
> **Herr Ober.** You might also be asked **getrennt oder zusammen?** (separately or together) if there are several people and you might want to split the bill. A service charge is usually included, but it is customary to add a small tip, for example Renate would probably have given 12 marks and said
> **stimmt so** – keep the change.

Key words and phrases

To use

Ist hier noch frei?	Is this seat free?
Haben Sie Kuchen/Torte?	Do you have any cake?
Was haben Sie auf der kalten Karte?	What have you got on the snack menu?
Die Speisekarte bitte!	The menu please!
Ich möchte etwas zu essen/trinken	I'd like something to eat/drink
Dann nehme ich . . .	I'll take . . .
ein Glas Milch/Saft/Wein	a glass of milk/juice/wine
eine Tasse Kaffee	a cup of coffee
ein Stück Kuchen/Torte	a piece of cake
ein Kännchen Tee	a pot of tea
ein großes/kleines Bier	a large/small beer

Mit/ohne . . .	With/without . . .
Milch	milk
Sahne	cream
Zitrone	lemon
Zucker	sugar

Herr Ober!	Waiter!
Fräulein!	Waitress!
Zahlen bitte!	The bill please!
Stimmt so!	Keep the change!

To understand

Was darf's sein?	Can I help you?

Möchten Sie	Would you like . . .
Brot oder Brötchen?	some bread or some rolls?
Kuchen oder Torte?	some cake?
ein weiches Ei?	a soft-boiled egg?
die Speisekarte?	the menu?
etwas zu essen/trinken?	something to eat/drink?

Wir haben . . .	We've got . . .
belegte Brote	sandwiches
verschiedene Salate	various salads

Getrennt oder zusammen?	Separately or together?
Ja, hier ist noch frei	Yes, (the seat) here is free
Nein, hier ist (leider) besetzt	No, (unfortunately) it's taken

And you often hear at mealtimes (and may want to use it yourself):

Guten Appetit!	Enjoy your meal! Bon appetit!

Practice what you have learned

This time it might be a good idea to read *Did you know?* on p. 61 *before* you do the listening exercises.

1 Look at this breakfast menu. Then listen to the tape. What is the woman going to have for breakfast? Write it down below. (Answers p. 62)

New vocabulary
Fruchtsäfte fruit juices
Eier im Glas soft-boiled eggs served in a glass
die Scheibe slice

Die Frau möchte ....

....

....

....

2 Listen to the tape. The waitress is just making out the bill. How much were the individual items? Write the prices down in the space provided. (Answers p. 62)

New vocabulary: **macht zusammen** . . . makes . . . altogether

a. eine Tasse Schokolade   .... , ... DM

b. eine Glas Tee   .... , ... DM

c. ein Käsetoast   .... , ... DM

d. ein Stück Erdbeertorte   .... , ... DM

e. macht zusammen   .... , ... DM

f. Did the guest give her a tip? If so, how much? ....

3 Some people are ordering snacks and drinks. What are they having? Listen to the tape and write down the items in the spaces provided next to the appropriate picture. (Answers p. 62)

New vocabulary: **die Salatplatte** salad platter

a.		
b.		
c.		
d.		
e.		
f.		

Grammar

Plural of nouns

The rules for forming the plural of German nouns are complex, but the following guidelines will help you recognize most of them. They either:

- add an **-e** (sometimes with an *Umlaut*) e.g.

    der **Tag** (the day)   die **Tage** (the days)
    die **Wurst** (the sausage)   die **Würste** (the sausages)
    das **Bier** (the beer)   die **Biere** (the beers)

- add **-er** (sometimes with an *Umlaut*) e.g.

    der **Mann** (the man)   die **Männer** (the men)
    das **Ei** (the egg)   die **Eier** (the eggs)

- add **-en** or **-n** (mostly feminine nouns) e.g.

    die **Frau** (the woman)   die **Frauen** (the women)
    die **Dusche** (the shower)   die **Duschen** (the showers)

- just add an *Umlaut* e.g.

    die **Mutter** (the mother)   die **Mütter** (the mothers)
    der **Vater** (the father)   die **Väter** (the fathers)

- don't change at all, e.g.

    das **Kännchen** (the pot, jug)   die **Kännchen** (the pots, jugs)
    das **Zimmer** (the room)   die **Zimmer** (the rooms)

- add an **-s** (mostly foreign words) e.g.

    das **Auto** (the car)   die **Autos** (the cars)
    das **Radio** (the radio)   die **Radios** (the radios)

Notice that the plural for 'the' is **die** with all three genders.

Good German dictionaries will always give you the plurals of nouns, and why not try to note all those you have met so far and those you meet from now on in the course.

Exercise Here are the plurals of some nouns you have already met. Complete the sentences below with the correct noun which you will find in the box below. (Answers p. 62)

a. Sprechen Sie auch andere ....?

b. Ich habe zwei ...., ich bin Student und Verkäufer.

c. Zum Frühstück möchte ich gerne zwei ....

    und zwei .... Kaffee.

d. Ich habe vier ...., zwei Söhne und zwei ....

e. Ich möchte gerne drei .... bleiben.

Tassen	Sprachen	Wochen	Kinder
Berufe	Töchter	Brötchen	

Read and understand

1 Tick the right boxes in the questions below. (Answers p. 62)

a. What would you order if you were very thirsty and wanted a non-alcoholic drink?

☐ Bier

☐ Weißwein

☐ Schnaps

☐ Zitronenlimonade

b. What would you order if you wanted a hot drink with just a bit of alcohol in it to warm you up?

☐ Tee mit Rum

☐ Kaffee mit Sahne

☐ Schokolade

☐ heiße Milch

c. What would you order if you were hungry and wanted something savoury? (2 possibilities)

☐ Käsesahnetorte

☐ Käsebrot

☐ Pommes Frites

☐ Brötchen mit Honig

2 Before you go on, practise some vocabulary in this crossword puzzle. The letters in 1, 2, 3, 4 will give you the name of an old German city, famous for its cathedral. (Answers p. 62)

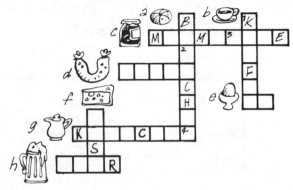

Did you know?

Snacks and drinks

Some snacks and drinks you'll find in Germany will be familiar to you –
hamburgers, hot dogs, fries (**Pommes Frites**), Coke (**Cola**), or even
Guinness – but many things are different.

Breakfast usually consists of rolls (or slices of bread or toast), butter and
jam (**Marmelade**) or honey (**Honig**). You can also ask for a soft-boiled egg
and assorted slices of sausage or cheese, but there are usually no cooked
items like bacon or scrambled eggs. Breakfast is served in most snack bars,
in cafés, pubs, hotels, and in the cafeterias of large department stores.

Coffee and tea The Germans prefer coffee to tea. You'll always be served
'real', i.e. ground coffee, even at the shabbiest kiosk, and it comes with a
small jug of evaporated milk. You'll find it almost impossible to get fresh
milk for your tea or coffee. Not many Germans have milk with their tea –
they prefer lemon or just have it black. A good (and cheap) cup of coffee
can be bought in special quick-service coffee bars owned by the major
coffee manufacturers. You just stand and sip your coffee – there's usually
no food.

Snacks Best known is **Bratwurst** (lit. fried sausage, but it's in fact roasted
on a charcoal grill), served with **Pommes Frites** or a roll plus mustard or
ketchup. **Bratwurst** is sold in open stalls or kiosks in the streets
(**Würstchenbude** or **Schnellimbiß**) or in snack bars (**Imbißstuben**). The
Bratwurst, however, has many foreign rivals nowadays, there are Italian
pizzas, French crêpes, Turkish kebabs, American pancakes, and, of
course, hamburgers. But **Fisch und Pommes Frites** don't seem to have
caught on yet. If you just want a cold snack you can buy one of the
numerous rolls or sandwiches with cheese, cold meat, ham, etc.

Drinks All kiosks and snack bars will serve alcohol as well as soft drinks. At
least there'll be beer (bottled) and **Schnaps** or brandy. The best place to go
for a drink though is a pub (**Gaststätte**, or **Kneipe**). Especially in big
cities you'll find a combination of pub/restaurant/café, often very cosy, with
imaginative decor, full of atmosphere and – sometimes – live music. You
can have a meal or just sit for hours with your **kleines Bier** – it's up to you.
The choice of beers, wines, spirits and liqueurs is enormous. We can't list
them all here, but you'll find some information on German wines in Unit
10. There are no licensing hours in Germany, Austria or Switzerland –
many pubs are open in the afternoons, and general closing time is between
midnight and one a.m., although many bars and even pubs are open even
longer.

Cafés Do not expect the equivalent of the American coffeeshop – German
(and Austrian and Swiss) cafés are much more luxurious with plush carpets,
tablecloths, soft chairs, and, of course, a variety of the most delicious **Torten**
and **Kuchen**. Cafés and coffee parlors (**Konditoreien**) can be quite
expensive. Bakeries (**Bäckereien**) sometimes have a back room where you
can have breakfast or a cup of coffee and a piece of cake for less money.

Your turn to speak

1 What would you say if. . .? Stop your tape after each question in English to give yourself time to think, give your answer in German, then wind on to compare it with the answer on tape. Repeat the exercise for a few times. You'll practice:

Ist hier noch frei?
Die Speisekarte bitte
Zahlen bitte
Stimmt so!

2 And now you order breakfast. You'll practice:

Ein Kännchen . . .
Mit . . .
Ein weiches Ei
Nein, danke!

Answers

Practice what you have learned p. 57 Exercise 1 Die Frau möchte ein Kännchen Tee mit Milch, zwei Brötchen mit Honig, zwei Eier im Glas, einen Orangensaft

p. 58 Exercise 2(a) 1,80 DM (b) 1,50 DM (c) 2,30 DM (d) 2,50 DM
(e) 8,10 DM (f) yes – 40 **Pfennige**

p. 58 Exercise 3(a) ein Glas Tee mit Zitrone (b) ein Brötchen mit Wurst
(c) eine Salatplatte (d) ein Kännchen Schokolade mit Sahne (e) ein Stück
Käsesahnetorte (f) eine Tasse Kaffee mit Sahne

Grammar Exercise p. 59 (a) Sprachen (b) Berufe (c) Brötchen, Tassen
(d) Kinder, Töchter (e) Wochen

Read and understand, p. 60 Exercise 1(a) Zitronenlimonade (b) Tee mit
Rum (c) Käsebrot *or* Pommes Frites

p. 60 Exercise 2(a) Brötchen (b) Kaffee (c) Marmelade (d) Wurst (e) Ei
(f) Käse (g) Kännchen (h) Bier. The name of the city is KÖLN
(Cologne).

5 Directions

What you will learn

- to ask where places are
- to understand the answers
- how to get about in a town
- to understand directions

and you will be given some hints about using public transport.

Study guide

	Dialogues 1–3: listen straight through without the book
	Dialogues 1–3: listen, read and study one by one
	Dialogue 4: listen
	Dialogue 4: listen and study notes
	Dialogues 5–7: listen straight through without the book
	Dialogues 5–7: listen, read and study one by one
	Dialogues 8, 9: listen without the book
	Dialogues 8, 9: listen, read and study one by one
	Study the *Key words and phrases*
	Do the exercises in *Practice what you have learned*
	Read the *Grammar* section
	Do the exercise in *Read and understand*
	Read *Did you know?*
	Do the exercises in *Your turn to speak*
	Listen to all the dialogues again straight through

Dialogues

1 *At the tram stop: Making sure you're going the right way*

Ruth	Sind Sie die Linie eins?
Fahrer	Ja.
Ruth	Fahren Sie zum Theater?
Fahrer	Ja.
Ruth	Die wievielte Station ist das?
Fahrer	Oh – die . . . fünfte Station.
Ruth	Gut. Und was kostet das?
Fahrer	Eins zwanzig.
Ruth	Bitte schön.
Fahrer	Danke!

◆ **die Linie** (tram) line, (bus) route
  der Fahrer driver
◆ **fahren** to go (by bus, tram, car, etc.), to drive

2 *Ruth asks where the tram goes*

Ruth	Fahren Sie nach Söflingen?
Fahrer	Ja, da ist Endstation.
Ruth	Gut. Danke schön.

die Endstation terminus

3 *Still at the tram stop*

Ruth	Fahren Sie in Richtung Donauhalle?
Fahrer	Nein. Gehen Sie bitte auf die andere Seite rüber.

4 *Announcements in the tram*

Theater!
Berliner Platz! In die Linien 2 und 7 bitte umsteigen!

der Platz square

frei

1 ▸ **fahren Sie zum Theater?** are you going to the theatre? More examples: **fahren Sie zum Bahnhof?** are you going to the station? **fahren Sie zur Hauptstraße?** are you going to High Street? Note that you use **zum** (to) with masculine and neuter and **zur** with feminine nouns (see *Grammar* section).

die wievielte Station? which stop? (**wieviel** = lit. how many) She could also
▸ have asked **welche Station?**

▸ **die fünfte** the fifth. To say fifth, sixth, etc. you just add **-te** to the numbers. There are only a few exceptions: **erste** (first), **dritte** (third), **siebte** (seventh), **achte** (eighth). From 20 onwards you add **-ste**: **zwanzigste, einundzwanzigste**, etc. You will find a full list of these ordinal numbers in the *Key words and phrases*.

2 ▸ **nach Söflingen** to Söflingen. Söflingen is a suburb of Ulm. **Nach** is the equivalent of 'to' if you go to a town or a country, e.g. **ich fahre nach London** (I go to London), **ich fahre nach England** (I go to England). You use **zum** or **zur** (see Dialogue 1) if you go to a street or building, e.g. **ich gehe zur Haupstraße/zur Bank/zum Bahnhof** (I go to High Street/to the bank/to the station). Note that you use **gehen** only if you *walk*; if you go by bus, train, car, etc. you always say **fahren**.

3 ▸ **in Richtung** in the direction of; towards.

Donauhalle a big building (hall) near the Danube.

gehen Sie bitte . . . please go . . .

auf die andere Seite rüber over to the other side.

4   **in die Linien 2 und 7 umsteigen** change for lines 2 and 7.

5 *At the Ulm tourist office*

Ruth   Wo ist der nächste Campingplatz bitte?
Frau Oswald   In Ulm haben wir leider keinen Campingplatz mehr; der nächste liegt zirka 35 Kilometer weg von Ulm, und zwar auf der Schwäbischen Alb zwischen Ulm und Reutlingen.

weg von away from
und zwar in fact; that's to say
zwischen between
Reutlingen town in Swabia
zirka approximately

6 *And where is the nearest post office?*

Ruth   Und wo ist die nächste Post?
Frau Oswald   Die nächste Post? Die ist neben dem Hauptbahnhof.
Ruth   Wie komm' ich zum Hauptbahnhof?
Frau Oswald   Vom Verkehrsbüro aus – eh – gehen Sie die Fußgängerzone ganz durch, und dann kommen Sie direkt zum Bahnhof. Fünf Minuten zirka.

♦ **die Post** post office

7 *How does Ruth get to Ulm-Jungingen?*

Ruth   Wie komme ich nach Ulm-Jungingen bitte?
Frau Oswald   Also Ulm-Jungingen, das liegt ziemlich nördlich von Ulm. Es gibt eine/es gibt keine gute Busverbindung dorthin. Da nehmen Sie bitte ein Taxi.
Ruth   Danke schön.

Jungingen a suburb of Ulm   **nördlich von** north of
ziemlich rather   **dorthin** (to) there

5   **in Ulm haben wir** . . . in Ulm we've got. . . . Note the word order again with the verb in second place (remember Unit 4: **dann nehme ich** . . .). The subject (**wir**) and the verb (**haben**) change places because **in Ulm** is at the beginning of the sentence. You could turn it round and say **wir haben in Ulm** . . .

♦   **keinen Campingplatz mehr** no campsite any more. **Kein** means 'no' when used with a noun. It follows the same pattern as **ein** and has to add **-en** here because the object of the sentence (**der Campingplatz**) is a masculine noun. Remember **ich habe einen Mann/Sohn** from Unit 2. 'I have no husband/son' would be **ich habe keinen Mann/Sohn.**

auf der Schwäbischen Alb on the Swabian Hills (a mountain range near Ulm northeast of the Black Forest).

6 ♦   **neben dem Hauptbahnhof** next to the main station. The **Hauptbahnhof** is always the biggest and most important station in a city. It's usually not only a mainline station but a station for the subway (**U-Bahn**) and local commuter trains (**S-Bahn**) as well.

gehen Sie die Fußgängerzone ganz durch go right to the end of the pedestrian mall. If it had been a street she would have said,

♦   **gehen Sie die Straße runter** go down the street. Note the position of **runter** – it comes after 'the street'.

fünf Minuten five minutes.

7 ♦   **es gibt** . . . there is; there are.

♦   **eine/keine gute Busverbindung** a/no good bus connection. Here you can see quite well how **kein** works. First Frau Oswald thinks there is a good bus connection and says, **es gibt eine gute Busverbindung**. But then she remembers that this isn't so and corrects herself: **es gibt keine gute Busverbindung**. It is **keine** (and not **keinen**) because **die Busverbindung** is feminine. More examples: **es gibt keine Sahne** there is no cream; **ich habe keine Tochter** I haven't got a daughter; **ich möchte keine Torte** I don't want any cake.

da nehmen Sie bitte ein Taxi then take a taxi (please).

8 *Asking the way in the street*

Ruth Entschuldigen Sie bitte, wo ist denn der Metzgerturm?
Mädchen Also, da gehen Sie jetzt geradeaus, und dann rechts, dann kommen Sie durch eine Unterführung durch und dann . . . links und dann . . . das nächste . . . also hundert Meter rechts.
Ruth Aha. Vielen Dank.

das Mädchen girl
♦ **geradeaus** straight ahead

9 *In Munich's pedestrian mall*

Ruth Und wo ist Schwabing bitte?
Junge Schwabing . . . ja, da nehmen Sie am besten die U-Bahn, weil das ein bißchen schlecht zum Laufen ist. Eh . . . gehen Sie grad vorne an den Stachus und . . . eh . . . nehmen Sie die U-Bahn. Das ist nicht schwer zu finden.
Ruth Danke schön.

der Junge boy   **ein bißchen** a bit, a little
weil because   **schlecht** bad

Munich's pedestrian mall

8

- **entschuldigen Sie bitte** excuse me please.

- **wo ist denn der Metzgerturm?** where's the Metzgerturm? The **Metzgerturm** (lit. butcher's tower) is a famous Ulm landmark. The word **denn** carries no special meaning – it's just a filler word.

  dann kommen Sie durch eine Unterführung (durch) then you'll come through an underpass. The second **durch** (through) at the end of the sentence is superfluous.

- **rechts** to the right.

- **links** to the left.

- **vielen Dank** many thanks.

9

Schwabing traditionally Munich's artists' and students' quarter, today more famous for its nightlife.

- **da nehmen Sie am besten die U-Bahn** the best thing is to take the subway.

- **zum Laufen** for walking.

  grad vorne an den Stachus (very colloquial) straight ahead to the Stachus. He should have said, **gehen Sie geradeaus zum Stachus**. The **Stachus** is a famous Munich square.

  nicht schwer zu finden not difficult to find.

Key words and phrases

To use

Entschuldigen Sie bitte! — Excuse me please!

Fahren Sie . . . — Do you go . . .
  zum Bahnhof? — to the station?
  zur Hauptstraße? — to High Street?
  nach Söflingen? — to/towards Söflingen?

Welche Station ist das? — Which stop is that?

Wo ist . . . — Where is. . .
  der nächste Campingplatz? — the nearest campsite?
  die nächste Post? — the nearest post office?
  Schwabing? — Schwabing?

Wie komme ich am besten . . . — What's the best way to get . . .
  nach Ulm? — to Ulm?
  zum Hauptbahnhof? — to the main station?
  zur Fußgängerzone? — to the pedestrian mall?

You might also need:

Ist das weit? — Is that far?

To understand

Gehen Sie bitte . . . — Please go . . .
  links — left
  rechts — right
  geradeaus — straight ahead
  die Straße runter — down the street
  durch die Unterführung — through the underpass

Der/die/das ist/liegt . . . — That's . . .
  100 Meter rechts — 100 metres (on your) right
  neben dem Hauptbahnhof — next to the mainline station
  in der Hauptstraße — in High Street

Nehmen Sie. . . — Take. . .
  ein Taxi — a taxi
  die U-Bahn — the subway
  die Linie 1 — no. 1 (tram line, bus route)
Es gibt eine/keine gute Busverbindung — There is a/there is no good bus connection
Umsteigen! — (All) change!

Ordinal numbers

Der/die/das

erste The first	**achte** eighth	**zwanzigste** twentieth
zweite second	**neunte** ninth	**einundzwanzigste** twenty-first
dritte third	**zehnte** tenth	. . .
vierte fourth	**elfte** eleventh	
fünfte fifth	**zwölfte** twelfth	**dreißigste** thirtieth
sechste sixth	**dreizehnte** thirteenth	. . .
siebte seventh	. . .	**vierzigste** fortieth
		etc.

Practice what you have learned

1   ? or ! Question or request? Listen to the tape, then put the right symbol in the box at the end of each sentence. (Answers p. 76)

New vocabulary
langsam slowly
immer always

a. Gehen Sie ins Theater ☐

b. Fahren Sie nach München ☐

c. Gehen Sie auf die andere Seite ☐

d. Gehen Sie auf die andere Seite ☐

e. Kommen Sie zum Museum ☐

f. Sprechen Sie langsam, bitte ☐

g. Gehen Sie immer geradeaus ☐

2   On tape you will hear a series of tramstops being announced. These have all been printed below in a box. Put them in the order in which they appear on tape by writing them in the spaces provided. (Answers p. 76)

a. ....

b. ....

c. ....

d. ....

e. ....

f. ....

Blücherstraße
Justizgebäude
Hauptbahnhof
Staufenring
Westplatz
Friedrich-Ebert-Straße

3 Which picture represents which dialogue? Study the routes marked . . . and listen to the tape. You will probably have to listen to each conversation several times! (Answers p. 76)

New vocabulary
fragen to ask   **breit** broad
die Ampel traffic light   **weiter** further
groß big

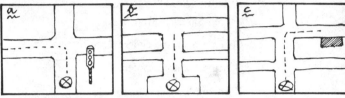

Karlstraße = Picture ....
Donauhalle = Picture ....
Museum = Picture ....

4 Listen to the tape where you'll hear a set of four directions relating to the map of central Freiburg below. Follow the directions one by one on the map, then write down where you'd finish up each time. Your starting point is at the bottom of Josefstraße (x). (Answers p. 76)

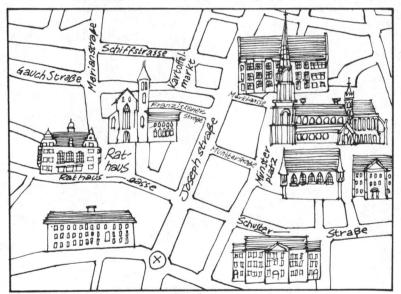

New vocabulary: **die Querstraße** crossroads

a. ....

b. ....

c. ....

d. ....

Grammar

Prepositions

Prepositions are useful words like 'on', 'at', 'to', 'in', etc. You have already met a few German prepositions in this course, especially in this unit, for example **nach** and **zu** (to), **durch** (through), **in** (in), **an** (at, by), **neben** (next to), **auf** (on). These words are short and quite easy to learn, but there is one snag: after prepositions the words for 'the' (**der/die/das**) and 'a' (**ein/eine/ein**) often change. In Unit 3 we explained the change from **der** to **den** and **ein** to **einen** called the *accusative case*, which happens to masculine nouns when they become the object of the sentence.

The same change from **der** to **den** and **ein** to **einen** also happens after certain prepositions, and here again we say that these prepositions 'take' the accusative case. For example, after **durch** (through):

Gehen Sie durch den Bahnhof Go through the station

Note again that there is no change for feminine and neuter nouns:
Gehen Sie durch die Straße Go through the street
Gehen Sie durch das Kaufhaus Go through the department store.

But not all prepositions take the accusative. Study the following sentences:

Ich bin auf dem/einem Platz (masculine) I am on the/a square
Ich bin neben dem/einem Haus (neuter) I am next to the/a house
Ich bin an der/einer Post (feminine) I am at the/a post office.

In this case **der** and **das** (masculine and neuter) have changed to **dem/einem**, and **die/eine** (feminine) to **der/einer**. This change is called the *dative case*, and in this unit it occurred after the prepositions **auf, neben, an** (see examples above) **zu**, and **in**. Some of these often use shortened forms, e.g.
an + dem = am
in + dem = im
in + das = ins
zu + dem = zum
zu + der = zur

What we have given you here is merely an explanation of certain patterns, to show you *why* it is sometimes **in** and at other times **im,** or why **am** sometimes changes to **an der**. At this stage simply be aware of these changes. You'll find more information about prepositions in the grammar summary on p. 225.

Read and understand

Read this extract from a prospectus issued by the Ulm tourist office. It tells you how to get to a nearby monastery (*Kloster Wiblingen*) Can you answer the questions below? (Answers p. 76)

Das Kloster Wiblingen liegt 4,5 km vom Ulmer Stadtzentrum. Busverbindungen: Vom Hauptbahnhof Ulm Linie 3 Richtung Tannenplatz oder Linie 8 Richtung Wiblingen. Ab Rathaus Ulm: Linie 4 Richtung Kuhberg, bei Haltestelle Ehinger Tor umsteigen in Linie 3 oder 8.

New vocabulary: **ab** from

a. How far is Wiblingen from Ulm town centre? ....

b. Where do you catch bus routes no. 3 and 8? ....

c. Which bus do you have to take first if you wanted to start off from the town hall? ....

d. What do you have to do when you get to Ehinger Tor? ....

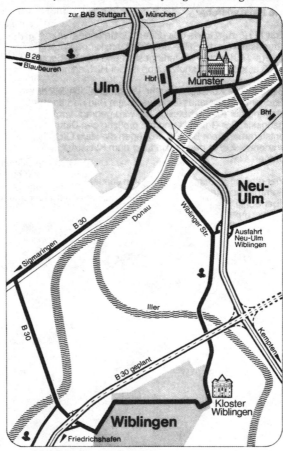

Did you know?

Getting around

If you are in a German town or city and want to find out about transport, it's best to go to the local tourist office (**Verkehrsbüro** or **Fremdenverkehrsamt**). Watch out for its symbol **i** (=**Information**). At many tourist offices you can also book rail or air tickets, theatre tickets, or even a package tour.

Means of transport

There are buses (**Bus** or **Autobus**) practically everywhere. Quite a number of towns and cities have still got trams (**Straßenbahnen**). In major cities you'll usually find suburban trains (**S-Bahn**) and/or underground trains (**U-Bahn**) as well.

Tickets and fares

The word for ticket is **Fahrschein** or **Fahrkarte**. You can buy a single ticket (**Einzelfahrschein**) or a ticket for several trips, which, depending on where you are, might be called either **Mehrfahrkarte, Streifenkarte** or **Sammelkarte**. They work out slightly cheaper than an **Einzelfahrschein**. Many cities offer special tourist tickets. As a rule you can use the same type of ticket on buses, trams, the subway and/or **S-Bahn**.

On most buses and trams there is no conductor, just the driver. You can buy a ticket from him when you get on, but it's best to buy it in advance from a ticket machine at the stop. There you'll also find information on fares. The further you travel, the more you pay, and you are supposed to work out your exact fare yourself according to an often elaborate and complicated plan with the fare stages (**Tarifzonen**) on it. To foreigners (and many Germans!) this can be a daunting task, and it's best to ask one of your fellow passengers for assistance.

Once you've got your ticket and are on the bus or tram or train, you must cancel your ticket, e.g. have it stamped by a little machine called **Entwerter** (canceller). The canceller is either inside the bus or tram or somewhere in the **U-Bahn** or **S-Bahn** station. The ticket is only valid if cancelled. There is no inspector or conductor on buses or trains or at the barrier, but there are spot checks to make sure you've got a valid ticket, and the fines for not having paid your fare are quite heavy.

Stops

These are called **Haltestellen**. There are different symbols for the stops of the various means of transport. The next stop is usually announced on a loudspeaker by the driver. Press a button next to the exit (**Ausstieg**) when you want to get off.

Your turn to speak

1 First, practice asking where various places are. You will use

Entschuldigen Sie bitte, wo ist . . .?

2 You want to find out where the museum is. You'll practice:

Entschuldigen Sie, wo ist . . .?
Ist das weit?
Wie komme ich. . .?

Answers

Practice what you have learned p. 71 Exercise 1(**a**) ? (**b**) ! (**c**) ! (**d**) ?
(**e**) ? (**f**) ! (**g**) !

p. 71 Exercise 2(**a**) Staufenring (**b**) Justizgebäude (**c**) Hauptbahnhof
(**d**) Friedrich-Ebert-Straße (**e**) Blücherstraße (**f**) Westplatz

p. 72 Exercise 3 Karlstraße picture (**b**), Donauhalle picture (**a**), Museum
picture (**c**).

p. 72 Exercise **4** (**a**) at the **Münsterplatz** (**b**) at the **Rathaus** (**c**) at the
Kartoffelmarkt (potatoe market) (**d**) at the **Marktgasse**

Read and understand, p. 74 (**a**) 4, 5 kilometres (**b**) at the **Hauptbahnhof**
(main station) (**c**) **Linie 4** (no. 4) (**d**) change for lines 3 or 8.

6 Time

What you will learn

- to ask what time it is
- to ask 'when'?
- to make statements on the time of the day
- to understand and use the words for the days of the week, the seasons, and the months of the year—
  and you will be reading about opening and closing times and holidays.

Study Guide

	Dialogues 1, 2: listen straight through without the book
	Dialogues 1, 2: listen, read and study one by one
	Dialogues 3, 4: listen straight through without the book
	Dialogues 3, 4: listen, read and study one by one
	Dialogues 5, 6: listen several times
	Dialogues 5, 6: listen and study notes
	Read the *Key words and phrases*
	Do the exercises in *Practice what you have learned*
	Read the *Grammar* section and do the exercise
	Do the exercises in *Read and understand*
	Read *Did you know?*
	Do the exercises in *Your turn to speak*
	Listen to dialogues 1–6 again straight through

Dialogues

□ **1** *What's the time?*

Ruth   Wie spät ist es?
Hannes   Zwölf Uhr.

□ **2** *What's the time now?*

Radio   Es ist zwölf Uhr drei.
Radio   Zwölf Uhr fünfundzwanzig. Drittes Programm.

Radio   Es ist fünfzehn Uhr.

□ **3** *At the museum in Ulm*

Ruth   Ist das Museum heute geöffnet?
Herr Schmidt   Ja, die Öffnungszeiten des Städtischen Museums sind täglich von
10 bis 17 Uhr, und das deutsche Brotmuseum hat täglich außer
samstags geöffnet, von 10 bis 12 und dann von 15 bis 17.30 Uhr.

- **heute** today
- **geöffnet** open (lit. opened)
- **täglich** daily

Deutsches Brotmuseum e. V.

gegr. 1955 von Dr. h.c. W. Eiselen,
Senator e.h. e.h.
7900 Ulm, Fürsteneckerstraße 17
Telefon 07 31 / 3 05 61

Geöffnet: täglich (außer samstags) von
10 – 12 Uhr und von
15 – 17.30 Uhr

1 ◆ **wie spät ist es?** what's the time?

◆ **zwölf Uhr** twelve o'clock. (**die Uhr** = clock)

2 ◆ **zwölf Uhr drei** three minutes past twelve (lit. twelve o'clock and three minutes). You say **zwölf Uhr drei** but you write **12.03 Uhr.**

◆ **zwölf Uhr fünfundzwanzig (12.25 Uhr)** twenty-five minutes past twelve; 12:25.

drittes Programm third program (e.g. of a radio station).

◆ **fünfzehn Uhr (15.00 Uhr)** 15 hours, i.e. 3 p.m. Note that for announcements, timetables, the speaking clock etc. the 24–hour clock is used. For example 5 minutes past midnight would be **0.05 Uhr** (pronounced **null Uhr fünf**), 3:20 a.m. is **3.20 Uhr (drei Uhr zwanzig)**, but 3:20 *p.m.* is **15:20 Uhr (funfzehn Uhr zwanzig)**. In everyday German, however, you use **3.20 Uhr** for 3:20 p.m. as well, but people usually say, **es ist zwanzig nach drei** it's twenty past three.

◆ **es ist zehn vor fünf** it's ten to five.

◆ **es ist Viertel vor sechs** it's a quarter to six.

◆ **es ist Viertel nach sechs** it's a quarter past six.

◆ **es ist halb sieben** it's half past six.

3 ◆ **die Öffnungszeiten** opening times.

das Städtische Museum municipal museum. (**Städtische** from **die Stadt** = town).

das deutsche Brotmuseum the German bread museum. This museum (in Ulm) charts the history of breadmaking through the centuries.

◆ **außer samstags** except on Saturdays. (**der Samstag** = Saturday)

◆ **das Museum hat geöffnet** the museum is open. You can also say **das Museum ist geöffnet**. Both forms are common.

◆ The opposite of **geöffnet** is **geschlossen** (closed).

4 *Ruth asks a bar owner about opening times*

Ruth   Wann sind Sie denn überhaupt geöffnet?
Frau Jahn   Wir haben die ganze Woche auf, nur montags haben wir Ruhetag.
Ruth   Und wann fangen Sie morgens an?
Frau Jahn   Um zehn.
Ruth   Und wann hören Sie auf?
Frau Jahn   Oh je, so zwischen ein und zwei Uhr nachts?

     überhaupt at all
◆ **nur** only
◆ **der Ruhetag** day off; closing day (lit. rest day)
◆ **um zehn** at ten
     oh je oh dear

5 *Holidays*

Ruth   Wann machen Sie Urlaub?
Frau Vollmert   Im nächsten Jahr mache ich zweimal Urlaub, im Frühjahr und im Herbst.
Ruth   Und was machen Sie da?
Frau Vollmert   Och, im Frühjahr möchte ich gern nach Griechenland fahren, da ist es noch nicht so heiß da. Ja, im Herbst, das weiß ich noch nicht genau, aber wahrscheinlich auch nach Südeuropa. Vielleicht im September oder Oktober nach Spanien, da ist es dann nicht mehr so heiß.

     Griechenland Greece
     heiß hot
     genau exactly
     wahrscheinlich, probably
     vielleicht perhaps
     nicht mehr no longer

4 ♦ **die ganze Woche** the whole week.

♦ **auf** open. The opposite of auf is **zu** (closed, shut). You'll often find these two words instead of **geöffnet** and **geschlossen.**

♦ **montags** on Mondays (**der Montag** = Monday). *All* days of the week are masculine.

wann fangen Sie an? when do you start? **Fangen + an = anfangen** (to start). The verb **anfangen** is separable, i.e. its two parts (**an** and **fangen**) are split. **Fangen** comes first and **an** goes right to the end of the sentence. More examples: **fangen Sie immer um zehn Uhr an?** (do you always start at ten?) **nein, wir fangen samstags um elf Uhr an.** (no, on Saturdays we start at eleven).

♦ Another useful word would be **aufmachen** (to open up). It follows the same pattern as **anfangen,** for example: **wann machen Sie auf? wir machen um zehn auf.** (when do you open up? we open up at ten).

♦ **morgens** in the morning. Similarly: **vormittags** (before noon), **mittags** (at noon), **nachmittags** (in the afternoon), **abends** (in the evening), **nachts** (at night). 'Seven a.m.' would be **sieben Uhr morgens,** seven p.m. **sieben Uhr abends; zwölf Uhr mittags** = twelve noon, **zwölf Uhr nachts** = twelve midnight.

wann hören Sie auf? when do you close? (lit. when do you stop?) **aufhören** (to stop) is another separable verb: **wir hören um ein Uhr nachts auf** (we close at one o'clock in the morning, lit. at night).

5 ♦ **wann machen Sie Urlaub?** when do you go on holiday? Note that **der Urlaub** (holidays; leave) is singular in German, just as 'leave' is in English.

zweimal twice. Similarly: einmal (once), **dreimal,** (three times), **viermal** (four times), etc.

♦ **im Frühjahr** in the spring (**das Frühjahr** = spring).
♦ **im Herbst** in the autumn (**der Herbst** = autumn).
♦ The other two seasons are **der Sommer** (summer) and **der Winter** (winter).

♦ **das weiß ich noch nicht** I don't know yet. (**nicht** = not, see *Grammar* section). Had she known when she was going, she'd have said, for example, **am fünften (5.) September** (on the fifth (5th) of September), **am ersten (1.) Oktober** (on the first) (1st) of October), see p. 84 for more details.

6 *A song about two seasons*

Drei Rosen im Garten
Drei Tannen im Wald
Im Sommer ist's lustig
Im Winter ist's kalt

die Rose rose
der Garten garden
die Tanne pine tree
der Wald the woods, forest
lustig jolly

Key words and phrases

To use

Wann . . .	When . . .
sind die Öffnungszeiten?	are the opening times?
hat das Museum geöffnet?	is the museum open?
ist das Restaurant auf?	is the restaurant open?
sind Sie geschlossen/zu?	are you closed?
machen Sie auf/zu?	do you open/close?
machen Sie Urlaub?	are you going on holiday?

To understand

Ich mache im Sommer Urlaub	I'm going on holiday in the summer
Das weiß ich noch nicht	I don't know yet
Zweimal im Jahr	Twice a year
Von 13 bis 14 Uhr	From 1 to 2 pm
Zwischen 12 und 15 Uhr	Between 12 noon and 3 pm
Um zehn	At ten
Nachts um zwei	At two o'clock in the morning
Vormittags	Before noon
Sonntags	On Sundays
Montag ist Ruhetag	Monday is our closing day
Wir haben die ganze Woche auf/zu	We are open/closed all week

Times

Wie spät ist es (bitte)?	What's the time (please)?
Es ist zehn Uhr	It is ten o'clock
Es ist fünf nach zehn	It is five past ten
Es ist zehn nach zehn	It is ten past ten
Es ist Viertel nach zehn	It is a quarter past ten
Es ist zwanzig nach zehn	It is twenty past ten
Es ist fünf vor halb elf	It is twenty-five past ten
Es ist halb elf	It is half past ten

Es ist fünf nach halb elf	It is twenty-five to eleven
Es ist zwanzig vor elf	It is twenty to eleven
Es ist Viertel vor elf	It is a quarter to eleven
Es ist zehn vor elf	It is ten to eleven
Es ist fünf vor elf	It is five to eleven

Days of the week

(der) **Montag** Monday
Dienstag Tuesday
Mittwoch Wednesday
Donnerstag Thursday
Freitag Friday
Samstag Saturday
Sonntag Sunday

am Montag on Monday
am Freitag on Friday

Months of the year

(der) **Januar** January
Februar February
März March
April April
Mai May
Juni June
Juli July
August August
September September
Oktober October
November November
Dezember December

im April in April
im September in September

Note ◆

der Tag day	**das Frühjahr** spring
die Woche week	**der Sommer** summer
der Monat month	**der Herbst** autumn
das Jahr year	**der Winter** winter

The date

Heute ist der . . .	Today is the . . .
erste (1.) September	first (1st) of September
dritte (3.) Mai	third (3rd) of May
vierundzwanzigste (24.) Dezember	twenty-fourth (24th) of December

but:

am . . .	on the . . .
ersten September	first of September
dritten Mai	third of May
vierundzwanzigsten Dezember	twenty-fourth of December

vom dritten bis zum zwölften Juli	from the third to the twelfth of July
vom vierzehnten bis zum siebzehnten April	from the 14th to the 17th of April

The shortest way of writing the date:

1.9.81	1/9/81
(der erste neunte einundachtzig)	(lit. the first of the ninth 'eighty-one)

The years:

neunzehnhundertzweiundachtzig	1982
achtzehnhundertfünf	1805

but

Das Jahr 2000 (zweitausend)	The year 2000

Practice what you have learned

1 Listen to the speaking clock on tape, and fill in the gaps. (Answers p. 90)

Beim nächsten Ton ist es . . . (At the tone it will be . . .)

a. .... Uhr   .... Minuten und .... Sekunden

b. .... Uhr   .... Minuten und .... Sekunden

c. .... Uhr   .... Minuten und .... Sekunden

d. .... Uhr   .... Minuten und .... Sekunden

2 Study the opening times of three famous sights in Ulm listed below. Then listen to the tape. Which sight is the dialogue referring to? (Answer p. 90)

Münster: täglich 9.00 – 17.00
Kloster Wiblingen: Dienstag – Sonntag 10.00 – 12.00 und 14.00 – 16.00
Aquarium: täglich 10.00 – 18.00; im Winter 10.00 – 17.00

3 On tape you will hear a short interview with Mr Schneider about his work and his holidays. Listen several times, then tick the right answers. (Answers p. 90)

New vocabulary: **jeden Tag** every day

a. Herr Schneider works

☐ every day

☐ four days a week

b. He doesn't work on

☐ Wednesday

☐ Monday

c. He works

☐ eight hours a day

☐ six hours a day

d. He always takes his holiday

☐ in the spring

☐ in the summer

continued next page

e. He goes away in

☐ July

☐ June

f. He goes away for

☐ two weeks

☐ three weeks

4 On tape you will hear a recorded message at Ulm station about train departures to Munich. Write down the departure times in the spaces provided. (Answers p. 90)

New vocabulary
der Intercity-Zug Intercity train
der D-Zug express train

a. Intercity-Zug ....

b. D-Zug ....

c. D-Zug ....

d. D-Zug ....

5 The recorded message from Exercise 4 also tells you the length of the journey from Ulm to Munich for various trains. Listen to it, then fill in the gaps below. (Answers p. 90)

New vocabulary
TEE-Züge *Trans Europ Express* trains
Schnellzüge fast trains
Eilzüge fast trains stopping frequently
die Fahrzeit length of journey
beträgt is (lit. totals)

Die Fahrzeit nach München beträgt:

a. für TEE- und Intercity-Züge ....

b. für Schnellzüge ....

c. für Eilzüge ....

Grammar

The use of 'nicht' (not)

The German word for 'not' is **nicht**. In simple sentences, it follows straight after the verb:

Sind Sie Frau Müller? Nein, ich bin *nicht* Frau Müller.
Are you Mrs. Müller? No, I am *not* Mrs. Müller.

Fahren Sie nach London? Nein, ich fahre *nicht* nach London.
Are you going to London? No, I'm *not* going to London.

Often you will see **nicht** in a different position, not after the verb, but at the end of the sentence or somewhere in the middle. Don't worry about it at this stage – just recognize **nicht** and know that this means a negative sentence. What you should be able to do yourself is to place **nicht** straight after the verb. Try the exercise below.

Exercise Answer the following questions – first with 'yes' and then with 'no'.
(Answers p. 90)
Example:

Gehen Sie zum Bahnhof? Ja, ich gehe zum Bahnhof.
Nein, ich gehe <u>nicht</u> zum Bahnhof.

a. Sind Sie aus Ulm?

Ja, ...

Nein, ...

b. Fahren Sie zur Donauhalle?

Ja, ...

Nein, ...

c. Arbeiten Sie in München?

Ja, ...

Nein, ...

d. Ist das Zimmer frei?

Ja, ...

Nein, ...

e. Ist das Verkehrsbüro weit von hier?

Ja, ...

Nein, ...

Read and understand

1 Study the different clocks and the expressions of time, then match them up.
(Answers p. 90)

A   B   C   D   E

a. halb vier ....

b. Viertel nach sechs ....

c. Viertel vor sechs ....

d. fünf vor zwölf ....

e. zehn nach neun ....

2 Here's a small extract from 'What's on in Hamburg.' It tells you the opening hours of some of the local museums. Study them, then read the statements below and tick off **Richtig** or **Falsch** (True or False).
(Answers p. 90)

KUNSTHALLE **Glockengießerwall** Die-So 10–17 Uhr Mo 10–19 Uhr	**AUTO-MUSEUM HILLERS** **Kurt-Schumacher-Allee** tägl. 10–18 Uhr
MUSEUM RADE **Naturpark Oberalster** Sa, So, 10–18 Uhr	**POST-MUSEUM** **Stefansplatz 1** Die-Fr 10–14 Uhr Do 10–16 Uhr

a. Die Kunsthalle hat täglich geöffnet   R   F

b. Das Museum Rade hat die ganze Woche geöffnet.   R   F

c. Die Kunsthalle hat Mittwoch auch abends geöffnet.   R   F

d. Das Post-Museum ist am Samstag und Sonntag geschlossen.   R   F

e. Das Auto-Museum hat am Montag Ruhetag.   R   F

f. Das Auto-Museum ist vormittags immer geöffnet.   R   F

Did you know?

Opening times and holidays

Here are some general guidelines on business hours. Slight variations from region to region are possible.

Shops

They usually open between 8 and 9 a.m. (Some baker's and butcher's open even earlier.) Shops shut either at 6 or at 6:30 p.m. from Mondays to Friday. Saturday closing times vary: in Germany shops shut at 1 or 2 p.m., except for the first Saturday of the month when most townshops are open till 6 p.m. for the **Langer Samstag** (lit long Saturday). In Switzerland and Austria the bigger shops tend to be open until 4 or 5 p.m. each Saturday. Alternatively they might offer late night shopping once a week. You'll find (especially in smaller towns and in the country) that shops are closed at lunchtime and in some regions one morning or afternoon, or even a whole day.

Pubs

Their hours vary considerably, but in general they open at around 11 a.m. and stay open till midnight or beyond.

Mealtimes in pubs and restaurants

Breakfast is served until 10 a.m., lunch from 12 to 2 p.m., dinner from 6 to 9:30; but many restaurants serve meals much later, and in many cafés (especially those catering mainly to students and young people) you can get breakfast till about 2 p.m.

Public holidays

These are called **Feiertage**. Many public holidays have religious origins and names. Predominantly Catholic **Länder** (federal states) sometimes have a holiday which is a working day in a 'Protestant' **Land** and vice versa. On some of these holidays there will be special events like processions, festivals, etc. You can ask the tourist offices for a list of forthcoming events, and most of the bigger towns and resorts publish a 'What's on in...' booklet. The local newspapers will also list what's on.

School holidays

These are called **Schulferien**. German schoolchildren get roughly the same number of days off as American pupils. Summer holidays are staggered from **Land** to **Land** in order to avoid chaos on the roads and railways, starting in June and generally ending by early September.

'Rosenmontag' (the Monday before 'Shrove Tuesday') is the highlight of the carnival season and a public holiday in many parts of Germany.

Your turn to speak

1 You'll be asked to repeat certain times of the day and some dates.

2 Imagine you're at a hotel reception desk and want to know about opening hours of the bar and the bank, and about breakfast time. You'll practice:

Wann ist/hat . . . geöffnet?
Wann sind die Öffnungszeiten?

Revision/Review

Now turn to p. 218 and complete the revision section on Units 4–6. On the cassette the revision exercises follow straight after this unit.

Answers

Practice what you have learned p. 85 Exercise 1(a) 12 Uhr 31 Minuten und 40 Sekunden (b) 12 Uhr 31 Minuten und 50 Sekunden (c) 12 Uhr 32 Minuten und 0 Sekunden (d) 12 Uhr 32 Minuten und 10 Sekunden.

p. 85 Exercise 2 The dialogue was about the **Aquarium**.

p. 85 Exercise 3(a) 4 days a week (b) Monday (c) 8 hours (d) in the summer (e) in July (f) 3 weeks

p. 86 Exercise 4(a) 12.55 (b) 13.05 (c) 13.28 (d) 13.46

p. 86 Exercise 5(a) 1 Stunde 14 Minuten (b) 1 Stunde 30 Minuten (c) 1 Stunde 45 Minuten

Grammar Exercise p. 87 (a) Ja, ich bin aus Ulm; Nein, ich bin nicht aus Ulm (b) Ja, ich fahre zur Donauhalle; Nein, ich fahre nicht zur Donauhalle (c) Ja, ich arbeite in München; Nein, ich arbeite nicht in München (d) Ja, das Zimmer ist frei; Nein, das Zimmer ist nicht frei (e) Ja, es (*or* das Verkehrsbüro) ist weit von hier; Nein, es ist nicht weit von hier.

Read and understand p. 88 Exercise 1 (a) D, (b) B, (c) C, (d) E, (e) A
p. 88 Exercise 2 (a) R, (b) F, (c) F, (d) R, (e) F, (f) R

7 Shopping (part 1)

What you will learn

- to ask for picture postcards, stamps and souvenirs
- to say that something is a bit too expensive, too big or too small
- to use metric weights when buying food
  and you will read about different kinds of shops and the post office.

Study guide

	Dialogues 1, 2: listen through without the book
	Dialogues 1, 2: listen, read and study one by one
	Dialogues 3, 4: listen without the book
	Dialogues 3, 4: listen, read and study one by one
	Dialogue 5: listen without the book
	Dialogue 5: listen, read and study
	Dialogue 6: listen without the book
	Dialogue 6: listen, read and study
	Study the *Key words and phrases*
	Do the exercises in *Practice what you have learned*
	Read the *Grammar* section
	Do the exercise in *Read and understand*
	Read *Did you know?*
	Do the exercises in *Your turn to speak*
	Listen to all the dialogues again straight through

Dialogues

☐ **1** *Looking for picture postcards*

Ruth	Verkaufen Sie auch Ansichtskarten von Ulm?
Verkäufer	Ja, hab' ich auch.
Ruth	Was kosten die?
Verkäufer	Pro Stück 40 Pfennig die normalen, und dann haben wir große für eine Mark und zwanzig.
Ruth	Aha. Dann nehme ich die zwei normalen bitte. Haben Sie auch Briefmarken?
Verkäufer	Die müssen Sie bei der Post holen.

☐ **2** *Buying souvenirs*

Ruth	Grüß Gott!
Verkäuferin	Guten Tag!
Ruth	Haben Sie auch Souvenirs?
Verkäuferin	Ja, wir haben Aschenbecher, und Weingläser. . .
Ruth	Aha. Was kostet denn dieses Weinglas hier?
Verkäuferin	Das kostet fünf Mark – das kleine –, und das größere fünf Mark neunzig.
Ruth	Hm. Und der Aschenbecher hier?
Verkäuferin	Der Aschenbecher ist aus Zinn und kostet dreizehn Mark fünfzig. Gibt es auch in kleiner, da kostet er neun Mark fünfundzwanzig.
Ruth	Ach ja, dann nehm' ich den kleinen Aschenbecher bitte.

♦ **das Souvenir** souvenir
der Aschenbecher ashtray

1 ◆ **verkaufen** to sell. Ruth could also have said, **haben Sie auch Ansichtskarten?** (do you also have picture postcards?)

◆ **die Ansichtskarte** picture postcard; **die Karte** = card (also 'ticket', see Unit 5, **Fahrkarte**), **die Postkarte** = postcard.

◆ **was kosten die?** how much are these?

die normalen the standard ones. There is no equivalent of 'ones' – just use the adjective (see also next note).

und dann haben wir große and then we have big ones.

◆ **Briefmarken** stamps, sing. **die Briefmarke; der Brief** = letter.

die müssen Sie bei der Post holen you must get them at the post office. Note the word order after **müssen** (must; to have to) – the second verb (**holen** = to get) goes right to the end of the sentence. More examples: **wir müssen nach London fahren** (we have to go to London), **sie müssen morgen arbeiten** (they have to work tomorrow).

2 **dieses Weinglas** this wineglass.

das kleine the small one.

das größere the bigger one.

(den) gibt es auch in kleiner there's also a smaller one.

dann nehm' ich den kleinen Aschenbecher then I'll take the small ashtray. Note that **der Aschenbecher** is the object here, and not only has **der** changed to **den** but the adjective **klein** to **kleinen**. See p. 224 for details.

3 *Ruth buys a small loaf of bread*

Ruth	Grüß Gott!
Verkäuferin	Grüß Gott! Was hätten Sie gerne?
Ruth	Ich möchte gerne ein Brot bitte.
Verkäuferin	Ein Brot? Wieviel? Ein Pfund, ein Kilo?
Ruth	Ein kleines.
Verkäuferin	Ein kleines, das wäre ein halbes Kilo.
Ruth	Gut.

das Pfund pound

4 *Buying fruit and vegetables in the market*

Ruth	Ein Pfund Pfirsiche bitte!
Verkäufer	Wir haben da verschiedene Pfirsiche, griechische, italienische, kleine, große.
Ruth	Griechische.
Verkäufer	Griechische . . . so, ein Pfund Pfirsiche.
Ruth	Ein Pfund Karotten.
Verkäufer	Ein Pfund Karotten.
Ruth	Und ein Pfund Kirschen.
Verkäufer	Ein Pfund Kirschen . . . da, ein Pfund Kirschen.
Ruth	Zwei Pfund Zwiebeln.
Verkäufer	Da hätten wir rote, weiße und normale Zwiebeln.
Ruth	Rote bitte.
Verkäufer	Rote . . .

der Pfirsich peach
die Karotte carrot
die Kirsche cherry
die Zwiebel onion

*Munich's 'Viktualienmarkt', one of
Germany's most famous markets* ◗

3   **was hätten Sie gerne?** what would you like (to have)? A polite form; she could also have said, **was möchten Sie gerne?**

♦ **ein Brot** a (loaf of) bread. No need to say 'loaf' in German. If you want to be more specific, you'd say **ein Weißbrot** (white bread), **ein Schwarzbrot** (black bread), or **ein Graubrot** (rye bread, lit. gray bread).

das wäre that would be.

ein halbes Kilo half a kilo.

4 ♦ **ein Pfund Pfirsiche** a pound of peaches. There is no equivalent of 'of' in German here; see also **ein Glas Wein, eine Tasse Kaffee,** etc.

♦ **griechische, italienische, kleine, große** . . . Greek, Italian, small, large . . .

♦ **rote, weiße und normale Zwiebeln** red, white and ordinary onions. Here are some more colors: **grün** (green), **blau** (blue), **gelb** (yellow), **schwarz** (black), **braun** (brown).
And you might like to buy some more fruit, for example:

♦ **ein Pfund Äpfel** a pound of apples.

♦ **ein Kilo Birnen** a kilo of pears.

♦ **zwei Pfund Trauben** two pounds of grapes. (See *Key words and phrases* for details on weights).

5 *At another shop*

Verkäuferin Guten Tag. Kann ich Ihnen etwas helfen?
Ruth Ja. Verkaufen Sie auch Souvenirs?
Verkäuferin Souvenirs eigentlich nicht – Gold- und Silberschmuck, und Steine vor allen Dingen.

6 *Ruth chooses a ring*

Verkäuferin Vielleicht ein Ring in Gold oder Silber?
Ruth Ja, das ist sehr schön. Haben Sie das auch in Gold?
Verkäuferin In Gold, ja, bitte. Sehen Sie – Gold mit Elfenbein.
Ruth Ja, der ist sehr schön. Was kostet der?
Verkäuferin Fünfundfünfzig Mark.
Ruth Ja, das ist mir etwas . . .
Verkäuferin . . . etwas zu teuer?
Ruth Ja, ein bißchen.
Verkäuferin Sehen Sie, der. Den finde ich auch sehr schön. Mit Bergkristall.
Ruth Ja, und der paßt.
Verkäuferin Der paßt sogar. Zweiundzwanzig fünfzig.
Ruth Ja, das ist ja sehr preiswert.

    mit Elfenbein with ivory
    mit Bergkristall with rock crystal
    sogar even
 ♦ **preiswert** cheap, reasonable

5   **kann ich Ihnen etwas helfen?** can I help you? **Etwas** here means 'a little' and is put into the sentence to make it sound more polite.

Souvenirs eigentlich nicht not really souvenirs.

Gold- und Silberschmuck gold and silver jewellery.

Steine stones; (**der Stein** = stone), here: semi-precious stones.

6 ◆ **das ist mir etwas zu teuer** that's a bit too expensive for me; **etwas** has two meanings, 'something' and 'a bit', e.g. **möchten Sie etwas kaufen?** (would you like to buy something?), **das ist etwas zu groß** (that's a bit too big). Another word for 'a bit' comes next.

  ◆ **ein bißchen** a bit. To say 'a bit of' or 'a little of' you can use both **etwas** and **ein bißchen: etwas Milch** (a little milk), **ein bißchen Zitrone** (a bit of lemon), etc.

  ◆ **den finde ich auch sehr schön** (short for **den Ring finde ich . . .**) I find this one very beautiful too.

  ◆ **der paßt** (short for: **der Ring paßt**) that (ring) fits. Again the noun (**Ring**) is omitted.

Key words and phrases

To use

Haben/verkaufen Sie (auch) . . .	Do you (also) have/sell . . .
Briefmarken?	stamps?
Souvenirs?	souvenirs?
Ansichtskarten?	picture postcards?
Das ist etwas/ein bißchen zu. . .	That's a bit too . . .
teuer	expensive
groß	big
klein	small
Der/die/das paßt	That fits
Das ist sehr preiswert	That's very reasonable
Dann nehme ich den/die/das	Then I'll take that one
Ein (halbes) Pfund/Kilo . . .	(Half) a pound/kilo of . . .
Pfirsiche	peaches
Karotten	carrots
Kirschen	cherries
Zwiebeln	onions
Äpfel	apples
Birnen	pears
Trauben	grapes

To understand

Wir haben . . .	We've got . . .
große	big
kleine	small
normale	ordinary
griechische	Greek
italienische	Italian . . . ones

Note: Weights and measures are metric in Germany, so a **Pfund** ($^1/_2$ kilo) is slightly heavier than an American pound. You buy fruit and vegetables in **Pfund** and **Kilos,** and also cheese, meat and sausage. You buy smaller quantities in grams (**Gramm**), e.g. **100 Gramm Käse** (100 grams of cheese).

Practice what you have learned

1 Listen to the dialogue a few times. It was recorded at an art gallery, and Ruth is enquiring about the price of cards, posters and pictures. Then answer the questions below. (Answers p. 104)

New vocabulary
da drüben over there   **das Plakat** poster
die Serie series   **das Bild** picture

a. How much is one card? ....

b. How much are the 12 cards altogether? ....

c. How much is the series of cards? ....

d. How much is a poster? (There are 3 prices) ....

....

e. The prices of the pictures vary from .... to .... DM

2 A customer is enquiring about postal charges. Below you'll find a list of his questions, and the official's answers jumbled up in a box. Match the questions and answers, then listen to the tape for the correct versions.

New vocabulary
mit Luftpost via airmail

a. Wieviel kostet ein Brief nach England?

....

b. Und was kostet eine Postkarte nach England?

....

c. Und ein Brief nach USA?

....

d. Ist das dann mit Luftpost?

....

e. Und ohne Luftpost?

....

> Das ist dann mit Luftpost, ja.
> Ein Brief nach England kostet 80 Pfennig.
> Postkarte nach England kostet 60 Pfennig.
> Bis 5 Gramm 1, 10 DM.
> 90 Pfennig.

3 At the market: How much are these vegetables and fruit per pound? Fill in the price tags while you listen to the tape. (Answers p. 104)

4 This riddle is all about a fruit. Can you guess which one? Listen to the tape several times.

New vocabulary
erst at first
wie (here) as
der Schnee snow

der Klee clover
das Blut blood
schmeckt allen Kindern gut all
    children like to eat it

Erst weiß wie Schnee,
dann grün wie Klee,
dann rot wie Blut –
schmeckt allen Kindern gut.

If you haven't guessed the answer, fill in this puzzle. Write down the German word for each food item. The encircled letters, read from top to bottom, will give you the answer to the riddle. (Answers p. 104)

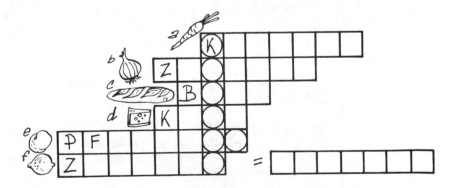

Grammar

Adjectives

Adjectives are words like **groß** (big, tall), **klein** (small), **grün** (green), **weiß** (white), **normal** (normal, ordinary), **teuer** (expensive), etc. They are used to describe things, e.g.

Der Apfel ist grün   The apple is green
Die Zitrone ist gelb   The lemon is yellow
Das Taxi ist schwarz   The taxi is black.

In sentences like these the adjective never changes – it's the same for masculine, feminine and neuter nouns. It doesn't change in the plural either:

Die Pfirsiche sind preiswert   The peaches are cheap.

But if adjectives come *in front* of the noun, there are certain changes. In this case you will find that they add endings like **-e, -er, -es, -en**, e.g.

der grüne Apfel   **den kleinen Ring**
ein schwarzes Taxi   **ein braunes Brot**
die preiswerten Pfirsiche   **ein kleiner Mann**, etc.

At this stage learn to recognize and use the *basic* adjective and don't worry about the changes. There is a list for your reference on p. 225.

Here is a list of some more useful adjectives:

alt old	**lieb** dear
arm poor	**lustig** jolly
bekannt famous	**möglich** possible
breit wide, broad	**nah** near
billig cheap	**naß** wet
dunkel dark	**neu** new
dumm stupid	**pünktlich** punctual
durstig thirsty	**reich** rich
eng narrow	**ruhig** quiet
fest firm	**rund** round
frisch fresh	**sauber** clean
furchtbar terrible	**sauer** sour
früh early	**schlecht** bad
glatt smooth	**schlimm** bad
glücklich happy	**schnell** quick, fast
hart hard	**schön** beautiful
heiß hot	**schwach** weak
jung young	**schwer** heavy; difficult
kalt cold	**sicher** safe; certain
kaputt broken, smashed	**stark** strong
krank sick	**trocken** dry
klug clever	**verrückt** mad, crazy
lecker delicious	**voll** full
leer empty	**wahr** true
leicht easy; light	**weich** soft

Read and understand

Below you will find a list of items on sale in a supermarket. Study the list, then tick the right boxes with either 'yes' or 'no'.
(Answers p. 104)

New vocabulary
Gurken (pl) cucumbers
die Packung packet
der Blumenkohl cauliflower

Griechische Pfirsiche 500g —.69DM	Gurken stück—.79 DM
Bananen 500g —.59DM.	Milkana Käsescheiben 150g Packung 1,59DM
Birnen 500g —.69DM	Amsterdamer Gouda 100g —.64 DM
Blumenkohl stück —. 99 D.M.	

With the items on sale . . .

a. Could you make a cauliflower cheese? yes ☐ no ☐

b. Could you make a fresh mixed salad? yes ☐ no ☐

c. Could you make a fruit salad? yes ☐ no ☐

d. Could you make apple pie? yes ☐ no ☐

Did you know?

Markets

Almost all towns, big or small, have one or two market days a week, often on Wednesdays or Saturdays. Some towns have a permanent market open from Mondays to Saturdays. At a market (**der Markt**) you can buy fruit and vegetables, flowers, herbs, eggs, cheese, meat, fish, bread – occasionally even wines and spirits. Besides offering an excellent choice, markets are usually good value too.

Supermarkets and other shops

In a **Supermarkt** you'll obviously find a good selection of cheese, sausage, bread, and other foods, including fresh fruit and vegetables. Toiletries can be bought there as well, and the choice of wines, spirits, liqueurs and beers is immense. There are also special shops where you can buy wines and spirits (**Weine und Spirituosen**), but they don't stay open at night. However, most railway stations have kiosks (**Bahnhofkiosks**) with "emergency" supplies of food and drinks.

Other useful shops are the **Metzgeri** (butcher's), **Bäckerei** (baker's), and the **Lebensmittelgeschäft** (general food store). If they are small and rather old fashioned, they're lovingly called **Tante-Emma-Laden** (lit. Auntie Emma's shop). Should you want to buy organic foods, ask for the **Bioladen** — or the more traditional **Reform haus.**

For newspapers, sweets, cigarettes and picture postcards you'll find the **Kiosk** very useful, a small hut with a little window which can be found in front of the station, at bus- or tramstops, or in the High Street. It has the advantage of being open very early in the morning, and often serves drinks and snacks as well.

The post office

This is called **Post** or **Postamt**. International calls can be made from any telephone booth marked with a green **International** or **Ausland** sticker. You can also go to the post office and book your call at a counter marked **Ferngespräche** (long-distance calls). The advantage is that you don't have to feed the telephone with coins, but can pay afterwards.

Your turn to speak

1 You're at the market buying fruit and vegetables. You'll practice:

Ein Pfund
Ein halbes Pfund
Drei Pfund

2 Now you're buying bread, some sausages and some cheese. You'll practice:

100 Gramm
Ein Weißbrot

Answers

Practice what you have learned p. 99 Exercise **1** (**a**) 1 mark (**b**) 10 marks
(**c**) 14 marks (**d**) 10, 24 and 30 marks (**e**) 315 and 75 marks

p. 100 Exercise **3** (**a**) 1.70, (**b**) 2.80, (**c**) 2.50, (**d**) 1.00

p. 100 Exercise **4** (**a**) Karotte (**b**) Zwiebel (**c**) Brot (**d**) Käse (**e**) Pfirsich
(**f**) Zitrone. The fruit is KIRSCHE (cherry)

Read and understand p. 102 (**a**) yes (**b**) no (**c**) yes (**d**) no

8 Shopping (part 2)

What you will learn

- more about buying food
- how to buy shoes and clothes
- how to ask for something for your aches and pains at the pharmacy
  and we'll give you some information on German drugstores and the health
  service.

Study guide

	Dialogue 1: listen through without the book	
	Dialogue 1: listen, read and study notes	
	Dialogues 2, 3: listen straight through without the book	
	Dialogues 2, 3: listen, read and study one by one	
	Dialogues 4, 5: listen without the book	
	Dialogues 4, 5: listen, read and study one by one	
	Study the *Key words and phrases*	
	Do the exercises in *Practice what you have learned*	
	Read the *Grammar* section	
	Do the exercise in *Read and understand*	
	Read *Did you know?*	
	Do the exercises in *Your turn to speak*	
	Listen to all the dialogues again straight through	

Dialogues

1 *At the cashier in the supermarket*

Verkäuferin Käse-Aufschnitt 125 Gramm 1.79
Magermilch Joghurt 50 Pfennig
Einen halben Liter Vollmilch 77
6 Flaschen Bier 4.49
Ein halbes Pfund Kaffee 6.99
Eine Teewurst 2.99
Ein halbes Pfund Butter 2.49
Eine Leberwurst 1.99
2 Flaschen Wein 0,7 Liter 2.99

der Joghurt yoghurt
die Leberwurst liver sausage
die Teewurst smoked sausage spread
der Käse-Aufschnitt assorted slices of cheese

2 *Buying a pair of sandals at the shoe store*

Ruth Guten Tag.
Verkäuferin Guten Tag. Bitte schön?
Ruth Ein Paar Sandalen bitte, Größe 36 bis 37.
Verkäuferin Und was für eine Art? Möchten Sie was Elegantes oder mehr sportlich?
Ruth Etwas Einfaches, Sportliches.
Verkäuferin Diese Art oder in dieser Art?

♦ **die Größe** size

3 *Trying the sandals on*

Verkäuferin Wie ist's mit der Größe?
Ruth Ja, fast ein bißchen zu groß. . . Ja, das ist jetzt besser. Das paßt.
Verkäuferin Hm, die Größe paßt Ihnen.
Ruth Und was kostet die?
Verkäuferin Die kostet 50 Mark – die ist im Sonderangebot.

fast nearly, almost
♦ **besser** better

1 die **Magermilch** skimmed milk (lit. meager milk); die **Vollmilch** =
unskimmed milk (lit. full milk).

♦ der **Liter** litre. All fluids are normally measured in **Liter** (**l**), e.g. **ein
halber Liter** (half a litre), **ein Viertel Liter** (a quarter of a litre), **dreiviertel
Liter** (three quarters of a litre). 1 litre = 1.7 pints.

zwei **Flaschen Wein** two bottles of wine. Note that there is no equivalent
of 'of'.

2 ein **Paar Sandalen** a pair of sandals. 'A pair of shoes' would be **ein Paar
Schuhe** (der **Schuh** = shoe). See p. 110 for shoe sizes.

und **was für eine Art?** and what kind? You can also just say
♦ **was für eine. . .?** for 'what kind': **was für eine Wurst möchten Sie?**
(what kind of sausage would you like?), **was für ein Auto haben Sie?**
(what kind of car have you got?)

♦ was **Elegantes** (short for **etwas Elegantes**) something elegant. Similarly:
etwas Einfaches (something simple), **etwas Sportliches** (something casual).

3 wie **ist's mit der Größe?** and how about the size? (lit. how is it with the
size?). 'What size?' would be
♦ welche **Größe?**

die **Größe paßt Ihnen** that size fits you.

und **was kostet die?** and how much is this one? **Die** refers to **die Sandale**.
The noun **Sandale** is omitted.

♦ die ist im **Sonderangebot** it's on sale.

Some clothes vocabulary you might like to know:
das **Paar Stiefel** (pair of boots), das **Paar Socken** (pair of socks), **das
Hemd** (shirt), die **Bluse** (blouse), die **Hose** (trousers), **der
Rock** (shirt), das **Jackett** (jacket)(men's), die **Jacke** (jacket)(women's),
der **Mantel** (coat), das **Kleid** (dress), der **Pullover** (sweater).

4 *At the pharmacy*

Apotheker Guten Tag, was darf es sein?
Ruth Haben Sie ein Mittel gegen Halsschmerzen?
Apotheker Ja . . . eh . . . dieses Präparat. Sie können vier- bis fünfmal täglich eine Tablette lutschen.
Ruth Also nicht mehr als fünf Tabletten pro Tag.
Apotheker Ja, zirka vier bis fünf Tabletten, und zwar lutschen, nicht schlucken.
Ruth Hm. Dann nehme ich die Tabletten hier.
Apotheker Danke schön.

der Apotheker pharmacist
das Präparat medication, medicine
lutschen to suck
⬩ **die Tablette** pill, tablet
schlucken to swallow
nicht mehr als no more than

5 *Still at the pharmacy*

Apotheker Sonst noch etwas?
Ruth Ja, Haben Sie ein Mittel gegen Insektenstiche?
Apotheker Ja, zum Einreiben – am besten ist die Lotion oder eine Creme.
Ruth Haben Sie auch ein Spray?
Apotheker Ein Spray haben wir auch.
Ruth Hmm – aber Sie finden die Lotion besser?
Apotheker Das Spray ist leider etwas teurer.
Ruth Aha. Dann nehme ich lieber die Lotion.
Apotheker Das macht 15 Mark 80 zusammen, bitte schön.
Ruth Bitte schön.
Apotheker 16, 18, 20. Danke schön.
Ruth Bitte schön. Wiedersehen.
Apotheker So. Wiederschau'n. Alles Gute. Recht schöne Reise.
Ruth Danke schön.

⬩ **die Lotion** lotion
⬩ **die Creme** cream
⬩ **das Spray** spray
⬩ **Insektenstiche** insect bites

4 **ein Mittel gegen Halsschmerzen** something for a sore throat; **das Mittel** = remedy (lit. means), **der Hals** = throat, **der Schmerz** = pain; **Schmerzen** = aches and pains. Similarly: **Kopfschmerzen** = headache; **Zahnschmerzen** = toothache. **Ich habe Kopfschmerzen** = I've got a headache (lit. I have headaches).

♦ *more useful words*: **die Reisekrankheit** = travel sickness, **die Krankheit** = sickness, illness; **ich bin krank** = I'm sick, I'm ill.

5 **sonst noch etwas?** anything else?

zum Einreiben to rub in.

♦ **am besten ist** . . . (the) best (thing) is . . . (see *Grammar* section)

♦ **teurer** dearer (from **teuer** = dear, expensive; see *Grammar* section)

dann nehme ich lieber . . . then I'd rather take . . . (lit. then take I rather)

Wiederschau'n (short for **auf Wiederschauen**) good-bye. In South Germany especially you'll often hear **auf Wiederschauen** instead of **auf Wiedersehen**.

♦ **alles Gute** all the best (lit. all good).

recht schöne Reise have a good journey.

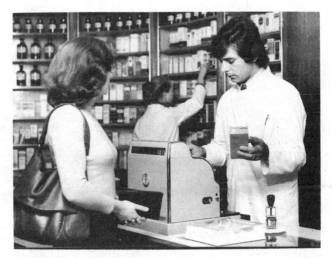

Inside an 'Apotheke'

Key words and phrases

To use

Ich möchte lieber etwas . . .	I prefer something . . .
Elegantes	elegant
Einfaches	simple
Sportliches	casual
Der paßt gut	This one fits well
Die paßt besser	This one fits better
Das paßt am besten	This one fits best
Ich habe Kopfschmerzen/	I've got a headache/a sore throat
Halsschmerzen	
Ich bin krank	I am sick/ill
Haben Sie ein Mittel gegen . . .	Have you got something for . . .
Halsschmerzen?	a sore throat?
Kopfschmerzen?	a headache?
Zahnschmerzen?	toothache?
Insektenstiche?	insect bites?
Reisekrankheit?	travel sickness?
Ich nehme die Tabletten	I'll take the pills

To understand

Was für ein. . .?	What kind of. . .?
Welche Größe?	What size?
Paßt der/die/das?	Does it fit?
Das ist ein/im Sonderangebot	That's a/on sale
Am besten ist . . .	Best is . . .
die Lotion	the lotion
die Creme	the cream
das Spray	the spray

Sizes of clothes and shoes

This is only a general guide. It is advisable to try things on before you buy them.

Men's clothes								
U.S./UK 34	36	38	40	42	44	46	48	50
Germany 44	46	48	50	52	54	56	58	60

Men's shirts						
U.S./UK 14	14½	15	15½	16	16½	17
Germany 36	37	38	39	40	41	42

Women's clothes								
U.S. 6	8	10	12	14	16	18	20	22
Germany 34	36	38	40	42	44	46/48	50	52

Shoes												
U.S.	3½	4	5	6	6½	7½	8	8½	9½	10½	11½	12½
Germany 33	34	35	36	37	38	39	40	41	42	43	44	45

Practice what you have learned

1 Back at the supermarket, the cashier is ringing up some more items and their prices. Studying the new vocabulary, then listen to the cashier and write down the prices next to the items. (Answers p. 118)

New vocabulary
das Mehl flour
Eiernudeln egg noodles
die Schokolade chocolate
die Zahnpasta toothpaste
die Rindfleischsuppe beef soup
Taschentücher handkerchiefs
die Seife soap
das Öl cooking oil

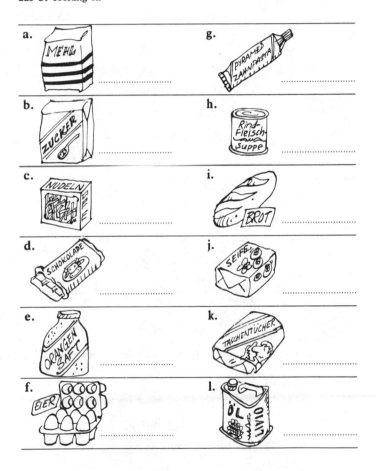

a. ....

b. ....

c. ....

d. ....

e. ....

f. ....

g. ....

h. ....

i. ....

j. ....

k. ....

l. ....

2 Sort out this shopping list by linking the correct weights and measures. Then listen to the tape and check if you were right.

Example

Amount	Item
200 g	Bier
1 Flasche	Eier
6	Käse

Amount	Item
200 g	Käse
1 Flasche	Bier
6	Eier

	Amount	Item		Amount	Item
a.	1 l	Trauben			
b.	1 Kilo	Taschentücher			
c.	1 Packung	Wein			
d.	1 kleines	Rindfleisch			
e.	½ Pfund	Sahne			
f.	¼ l	Brot			

g = gram

l = litre

3 Listen to the tape. Can you guess what's being advertised in a big department store? You will hear a short ad for some items of clothing. Tick the right boxes for the questions below. (Answers p. 118)

New vocabulary
meine Damen und Herren ladies and gentlemen
schick chic, fashionable

a. Are the items advertised on sale? yes ☐ no ☐

b. What's being advertised for ladies? blouses ☐ skirts ☐

c. And for gentlemen? jackets ☐ trousers ☐

d. What is the lowest price for the ladies'

items? 20DM ☐ 10DM ☐

e. And for the gentlemen's items? 65DM ☐ 75DM ☐

4 Listen to the conversation between Ruth and a saleslady. Ruth wants to buy a skirt. She tries one on – it fits and she takes it. Try to write a short version of the conversation by completing the speech bubbles in the pictures. Be as brief as possible, as we have shown you in pictures **a** and **b**. (Answers p. 118)

New vocabulary
verschiedene Modelle various kinds of skirts
probieren to try on
selbstverständlich of course

5 Listen to the pharmacist's recommendations on tape, then tick the right boxes. (Answers p. 118)

a. The best thing to take is

☐ tablets

☐ a lotion

☐ an ointment

b. You are supposed to take it

☐ three times a day

☐ twice a day

☐ once a day

c. You have to take it for about

☐ a week

☐ a month

☐ two weeks

d. If you aren't better you should

☐ come again

☐ see a doctor

☐ try another medicine

Grammar

More about adjectives

gut   besser am besten
good   better best

You have already come across the above comparisons in the dialogues. As in English, they are irregular. Here are some examples of their use in a sentence:

Diese Tabletten sind am besten. These tablets are best.
Wie komme ich am besten zum Bahnhof? What's the best way to get to the station?
Was ist besser, eine Creme oder eine Lotion? What's better, a cream or a lotion?

Most other adjectives are regular:

klein kleiner am kleinsten
small smaller smallest

Example: **Dieses Kind ist klein.** This child is small.
Dieses Kind ist kleiner. This child is smaller.
Dieses Kind ist am kleinsten. This child is smallest.

Here are some more examples:

cheap	**billig**	**billiger**	**am billigsten**
beautiful	**schön**	**schöner**	**am schönsten**
short	**kurz**	**kürzer***	**am kürzesten*****
long	**lang**	**länger***	**am längsten**
big	**groß**	**größer***	**am größten**
expensive	**teuer**	**teurer****	**am teuersten**
young	**jung**	**jünger***	**am jüngsten**

    * note the **Umlaut**
  ** note that the 'e' is dropped } for easier pronunciation
*** note that an 'e' is added

As with the *basic* adjective (see Unit 7, p. 101), comparative adjectives can change their endings when they come in front of the noun. Just learn the basic comparative at this stage. The **am** in the third form (superlative) is also dropped when in front of a noun: **die teuersten Geschäfte** (the most expensive shops), **die besten Tabletten** (the best pills).

Read and understand

Study the advertisements below. One doesn't make sense. Can you spot it?
Then answer the questions. (Answers p. 118)

New vocabulary
die Baumwolle cotton
die Wolle wool

How much would you have to pay

a. for a ladies' T-shirt? ....

b. for a girl's skirt? ....

c. for a men's shirt? ....

d. for a pair of children's shorts? ....

Did you know?

Pharmacies

At the pharmacy (**die Apotheke**) drugs and medicines are dispensed. Some drugs require no doctor's prescription, others do. But you might find what is on prescription and what isn't different from the US regulations. Drugs are generally cheaper on prescription, but you obviously have to see a doctor. You can also buy cosmetics and some health foods in an **Apotheke**.

A **Drogerie** will sell some drugs, but is mainly for toiletries, cosmetics, film, etc. A posher (and more expensive) version of the **Drogerie** is the **Parfümerie** where you can get mainly perfumes and cosmetics.

Doctors and hospitals

A general practitioner is called **Praktischer Arzt**. If he can't help you he'll refer you to a specialist (**Facharzt**) rather than sending you to a hospital. In emergencies there is of course the hospital (**Krankenhaus** ar **Spital** in Austria); the outpatient clinic is called **Ambulanz**.

More about shops

Department stores are called **Kaufhaus** or **Warenhaus** and obviously offer the most comprehensive choice. Famous department chain stores are **Kaufhof, Hertie, Horten, Karstadt** and **Kepa** in Germany, **Kastner und öhler** in Austria, and **Migros, Globus,** and **Jemali** in Switzerland, and you'll find a Woolworth in most big cities. **Kaufhäuser** (and many other shops, cafés and restaurants) are often situated in the **Fußgängerzone** (pedestrian mall). Many German towns have such areas these days, often attractively laid out with trees, benches, street cafés, market stalls, etc.

Your turn to speak

1 You're at the pharmacy. You'll practice:

Ich habe . . . schmerzen
Haben Sie ein Mittel gegen . . .?
3 mal täglich

Answers

Practice what you have learned p. 111 Exercise 1(a) 79 (Pfennig) (b) 1, 47
(c) 79 (d) 1,28 (e) 1,68 (f) 1,56 (g) 2,49 (h) 1 Mark (i) 1,39 (j) 99
(k) -,79 (l) 2,99

p. 112 Exercise 3(a) yes (b) blouses (c) trousers (d) 20 DM (e) 75 DM

p. 113 Exercise 4(c) gut (d) (Größe) 36 (e) Was kostet der Rock?
(f) Kann ich mit Scheck bezahlen?

p. 114 Exercise 5(a) tablets (b) three times a day (c) a week (d) see a
doctor

Read and understand p. 116. The advertisement **Herren-Pullover für
kleine Mädchen** (gents' pullovers for little girls) doesn't make sense.
(a) 15 marks (b) 9 marks (c) 9 marks (d) 5 marks

9 Making travel arrangements

What you will learn

- to buy a train ticket (one way, round trip, first and second class)
- to find out the best way of getting where you want to go
- to understand train announcements
- to understand and enquire about timetables

and you will also be given some information on air travel, and some general advice on travelling in the German-speaking countries.

Study guide

	Dialogues 1, 2: listen straight through without the book	
	Dialogues 1, 2: listen, read and study notes	
	Dialogues 3, 4: listen straight through without the book	
	Dialogues 3, 4: listen, read and study one by one	
	Dialogues 5–7: listen straight through without the book	
	Dialogues 5–7: listen, read and study one by one	
	Dialogues 8, 9: listen only	
	Dialogues 8, 9: listen, read and study notes	
	Study the *Key words and phrases*	
	Do the exercises in *Practice what you have learned*	
	Read the *Grammar* section	
	Do the exercises in *Read and understand*	
	Read *Did you know?*	
	Do the exercises in *Your turn to speak*	
	Listen to all the dialogues once again straight through	

Dialogues

☐ 1 *A train has arrived at Ulm station*

Loudspeaker Hier Ulm Hauptbahnhof, Ulm Hauptbahnhof. Intercity 518 'Patrizier' von München nach Hamburg-Altona. Über Stuttgart, Heidelberg, Mannheim, Bonn, Köln, Düsseldorf, Dortmund, Osnabrück. Planmäßige Abfahrt 8.59 Uhr.

über via
♦ **planmäßige Abfahrt** scheduled departure

☐ 2 *Connections*

Loudspeaker Sie haben Anschluß zum Eilzug nach Aalen über Langenau, Niederstotzingen, Sontheim, Gingen, Heidenheim. Planmäßige Abfahrt 9.05 Uhr Gleis 7.

♦ **das Gleis** platform (lit. track)

☐ 3 *Buying a ticket at the ticket office*

Beamtin Guten Tag. Bitte schön?
Fahrgast Nach Augsburg einfach, bitte.
Beamtin Erster oder zweiter Klasse?
Fahrgast Zweiter Klasse.
Beamtin Zweiter Klasse – kostet 12 Mark, bitte.

der Fahrgast passenger (male and female)

☐ 4 *A classy customer*

Fahrgast Eine Fahrkarte nach München bitte.
Beamtin Wann kommen Sie denn wieder zurück?
Fahrgast In 14 Tagen.
Beamtin Wollen Sie erster Klasse, zweiter Klasse, oder. . .?
Fahrgast Erster Klasse natürlich, und mit Intercity.
Beamtin Kostet 64 Mark, und 20 Mark der Intercity-Zuschlag.

IC 518
Patrizier
München-Stuttgart-Köln-Hamburg

1 ◆ All Intercity trains have names, this one is called **Patrizier** (patrician).
Altona is the name of a big station in Hamburg.

8.59 Uhr 8:59. You say **8 Uhr 59**, but you write **8.59 Uhr.**

2 ◆ **Sie haben Anschluß zum . . .** you've got a connection to . . .

Aalen is a town north of Ulm, and all the other towns mentioned in the
dialogue are stops *en route* to **Aalen.**

3 ◆ **einfach, bitte** one way, please. 'Round trip to Augsburg, please' would be
◆ **nach Augsburg hin und zurück, bitte.**

◆ **erster oder zweiter Klasse?** first or second class?

4 ◆ **die Fahrkarte** ticket. Similarly: **die Platzkarte** = seat reservation; (lit. seat
card), **die Rückfahrkarte** − round-trip ticket, **die Kinderfahrkarte** =
children's ticket, **die Sonderfahrkarte** = special ticket.

wann kommen Sie denn wieder zurück? when will you be coming back
again? Apparently he's buying a round-trip ticket, but there are different
rates depending on how long you're staying away. That's why she's asking
him when he's coming back. There are all sorts of special reductions – ask at
the German Tourist Office.

◆ **der Intercity-Zuschlag** Intercity surcharge. 20 marks is the surcharge for a
first-class return journey; it's 10 marks for a one-way trip. If you go second−
class, you have to pay 5 marks one way and 10 marks round trip.

☐ **5** *At the information desk at Ulm station*

Fahrgast Können Sie mir sagen, wann der nächste Zug nach Hamburg fährt?

Beamtin Ja, Sie haben Glück. Um 10.59 Uhr können Sie direkt nach Hamburg fahren. In Hamburg-Hauptbahnhof 20.21.

☐ **6** *Asking the best way to get somewhere*

Fahrgast Guten Tag. Wie komme ich am besten nach Neuschwanstein, bitte?

Beamtin An welchem Tag und ab wieviel Uhr wollen Sie fahren?

Fahrgast An einem Sonntag, ungefähr um 9 Uhr.

Beamtin Gut, dann fahren Sie in Ulm ab um 9.01 Uhr, in Kempten 10.26 Uhr, dann geht's weiter mit einem Bus um 11.05 Uhr, und 12.25 Uhr in Füssen.

ungefähr approximately.

☐ **7** *When's the last train back?*

Fahrgast Sehr gut. Und wann fährt der letzte Zug zurück?

Beamtin In Füssen ab 18.53 Uhr, in Augsburg 21.03 Uhr, ab 21.14 Uhr, und 21.57 in Ulm.

5 **können Sie mir sagen. . .?** could you tell me. . .? A polite way of asking a
♦ question. He could also have asked, **wann fährt der nächste Zug nach
Hamburg?** when's the next train to Hamburg?

Sie haben Glück you are lucky; (lit. you have luck; **das Glück** = luck)

6 **Neuschwanstein** a castle in Bavaria, built by the Bavarian king Ludwig II
in the last century.

♦ **an welchem Tag?** on which day?

ab wieviel Uhr? from what time (on)? Or, simpler: **um wieviel Uhr?** (at
what time?)

dann fahren Sie in Ulm ab um 9.01 Uhr then you'll leave Ulm at 9.01;
fahren . . . ab from **abfahren** – to leave, to depart. **Abfahren** is separable:
ich fahre ab (I'm leaving), **ich fahre in Ulm ab** (I'm leaving from Ulm).
See also **die Abfahrt** = departure.

dann geht's weiter (short for **dann geht es weiter**) then you go on.

Füssen the nearest town to Neuschwanstein.

7 **in Füssen ab 18.53 Uhr** departing Füssen 18.53 **Ab** here comes from
abfahren.

In Augsburg 21.03 Uhr arriving in Augsburg 21.03. Sometimes you'll find
Augsburg an 21.03; an comes from **ankommen** (to arrive; see also
♦ **die Ankunft** = arrival). Make sure you know the difference between
an and **ab**, e.g.
♦ **in Ulm ab** leaves Ulm
♦ **in Ulm an** arrives Ulm.

| | 8 | *Back on the platform* |

Loudspeaker Am Gleis 2 bitte einsteigen. Türen schließen selbsttätig. Vorsicht bei der Abfahrt.

There is no need for you to use these phrases but make sure you understand them.

♦ **am Gleis 2 bitte einsteigen** please board the train at platform 2.

Türen schließen selbsttätig doors shut automatically.

Vorsicht bei der Abfahrt stand clear, the train is about to leave (lit. caution during departure).

| | 9 | *Fräulein Beier enquires at a travel agent about travelling from Ulm to Berlin by plane.* |

Frau Hildesheim Flugzeug – ist der nächste Flughafen Stuttgart. Ab Stuttgart um 9 Uhr zum Beispiel. Die Maschine verkehrt täglich außer sonntags. Wann soll die Reise denn sein?

Frl. Beier Ja, am Wochenende.

Frau Hildesheim 9 Uhr – oder um 12 Uhr ist ein Abflug, oder 15.20 Uhr – die Flugzeit ist genau eine Stunde.

♦ **das Flugzeug** ⎫
♦ **die Maschine** ⎬ aeroplane
♦ **das Wochenende** weekend
    die Flugzeit flying time

ist der nächste Flughafen Stuttgart. Very colloquial. She should have said
♦ **der nächste Flughafen ist Stuttgart** the nearest airport (for Ulm) is Stuttgart.

die Maschine verkehrt täglich there are daily flights (lit. the plane runs daily).

wann soll die Reise denn sein? when would you like to travel? (lit. when shall the journey be?) **denn** is a fill word and carries no special meaning.

♦ **um 12 Uhr ist ein Abflug** there is a departure at 12 o'clock.

For more air travel vocabulary see *Key words and phrases*.

Key words and phrases

Travelling by train

To use

die Fahrkarte	ticket
das Gleis	platform
Nach Augsburg . . .	To Augsburg . . .
einfach bitte	one way, please
hin und zurück bitte	round trip, please
Einmal/zweimal Augsburg einfach	One/two one way(s) to Augsburg
Erster/zweiter Klasse bitte	First/second class, please
Wann fährt der nächste Zug nach. . . ?	When's the next train to. . .?
Wie komme ich am besten nach. . .?	What's the best way to. . .?
Ich möchte gerne. . .	I'd like to . . .
am Wochenende fahren	go on the weekend
am Sonntag reisen	travel on Sunday

To understand

Sie haben Anschluß (zum Zug) nach . . .	There is a connection to . . .
Planmäßige Abfahrt/Ankunft 12.05	Scheduled departure/arrival 12:05
(In) Ulm an/ab 19.40	Arrives/departs Ulm 19:40
5 DM Intercity-Zuschlag	5 marks Intercity surcharge
Wann möchten Sie fahren?	When would you like to travel?
An welchem Tag und um wieviel Uhr?	What day and what time?

Travelling by plane

Of course you can always get by in English at airports, but there are a few phrases you should know in German, such as:

der Flug	flight
der Abflug	departure
die Ankunft	arrival
das Flugticket/der Flugschein	air ticket
der Flughafen	airport
Wann ist der nächste Flug?	When's the next flight?
Wann fliegt die nächste Maschine?	When's the next plane?
Ich möchte gerne . . .	I'd like to . . .
am Wochenende fliegen	fly on the weekend
einen Flug buchen	book a flight

Practice what you have learned

1 A train is pulling into Ulm Station. Listen to the announcement on tape and answer the questions below. (Answers p. 132)

a. What is the number of the platform? ....

b. What kind of train is it? ....

c. Would you have to pay extra for travelling on this train?

....

d. Can you work out the train's route? Listen carefully, then mark the route on the map.

2 Again you'll hear some announcements at a station after a train has arrived. Three connections are announced on the loudspeaker. What kind of trains are they, where do they go, when do they leave and from which platform? Listen to the announcement, then fill in the grid below. (We've filled in the first **Anschluß** for you). (Answers p. 132)

	Zug	nach	Abfahrt	Gleis
a.	Eilzug	Regensburg	11.20	28
b.				
c.				

3 This announcement was made on a train, a few minutes before it was due to arrive in Munich. What does it say? Listen to the announcement on your cassette and fill in the gaps. The missing words are jumbled-up below. (Answers p. 132)

New vocabulary
erreichen to reach
wird bereitgestellt will be waiting

Meine Damen und Herren, in wenigen Minuten erreichen wir

....

Dort haben Sie Anschluß zum 181

nach Mittenwald.

Dieser .... wird bereitgestellt auf

.... 25.

4 This dialogue is about train connections from Ulm to Berlin-Zoo, West Berlin's main station. Listen to the tape, and make your notes on this form. We have filled in the stations for you. Can you fill in the arrival and departure times and the various fares in the gaps below? (Answers p. 132)

New vocabulary
der Liegewagen couchette
der Schlafwagen sleeper
der Preis price

Reiseverbindungen
Connections
Horaires des relations

(Auskunft ohne Gewähr)
(Information without guarantee)
(Information sans garantie)

Reisetag/Wochentag date/day date/jours Station ▼	►	Uhr time heure	Uhr time heure	Uhr time heure	Uhr time heure	Bemerkungen notes observations
Ulm	ab dep					
Donauwörth	an arr					
11	ab dep					
Berlin-Zoo	an arr					
	ab dep					
	an arr					
	ab dep					
	an arr					
	ab dep					
	an arr					

600 01 (neu) Merkzettel für Fahrplanauskünfte A6q Bk100 5c60 München VII75 100 000 M 2001   2.3.4.5.6.7.8.9.10./75.76.77.78.

Preis: .... DM für eine Fahrkarte .... Klasse

nach Berlin-Zoo. Liegewagen: zirka .... DM

Schlafwagen: zirka .... DM

5 A young man goes into a travel agent's to enquire about fares to London. Listen to the conversation. Are the statements below True or False? (**Richtig oder Falsch?**) Tick the right box. (Answers p. 132)

a. The young man wants to go to Düsseldorf ☐ R ☐ F

b. He'd rather go by train ☐ R ☐ F

c. There are quite a few cheap flights ☐ R ☐ F

d. There is a weekend reduction from Düsseldorf airport ☐ R ☐ F

e. DM 280 is the single fare only ☐ R ☐ F

f. He wants to book a flight at once ☐ R ☐ F

Grammar

Some modal verbs (can, must, etc.)

Verbs like **müssen** (must, to have to . . . do something), **können** (can, to be able to . . . do something) or **wollen** (to want to . . . do something) are called *modal* verbs. In most cases they cannot be used on their own. There has to be another verb in the sentence, e.g. **wir müssen jetzt gehen** (we must go now), **können Sie morgen kommen?** (can you come tomorrow?).

As in English, these verbs are irregular. Here is a list of the modal verbs you have met so far in their present tense, plus some examples of how they occurred in the dialogues or notes.

müssen

ich muß	I must	**wir müssen**	we must
du mußt	you must	**ihr müßt**	you must
er, sie, es muß	he, she, it must	**Sie/sie müssen**	you/they must

Wann muß ich abfahren? When do I have to leave?
Dann müssen Sie umsteigen. Then you have to change.

wollen

ich will	I want to (*not* 'I will')	**wir wollen**	we want to
du willst	you want to	**ihr wollt**	you want to
er, sie, es will	he, she, it wants to	**Sie/sie wollen**	you/they want to

An welchem Tag wollen Sie fahren? What day do you want to go?
Ich will an einem Sonntag fahren. I want to go on a Sunday.

können

ich kann	I can	**wir können**	we can
du kannst	you can	**ihr könnt**	you can
er, sie, es kann	he, she, it can	**Sie/sie können**	you/they can

Können Sie mir sagen, wann der nächste Zug fährt? Can you tell me when the next train goes?
Kann ich Ihnen helfen? Can I help you?

Note that after all forms of **müssen, wollen, können** etc. the second verb goes to *the end of the sentence.*

Another modal verb you are already familiar with is **möchten.** (**Was möchten Sie?** What would you like?). As you know from Unit 3, **möchten** is sometimes used on its own *without* a second verb:

Ich möchte ein Eis (haben) I'd like (to have) an ice cream
Möchten Sie ein Zimmer (haben)? Would you like (to have) a room?

Some other modal verbs can also be used on their own if the meaning of the sentence is clear. In English this is not possible.

Ich will zum Hauptbahnhof (fahren). I want to go to the station.
Ich muß ins Büro (gehen). I have to go to the office.
Sie kann Englisch (sprechen). She can speak English.

Read and understand

1 Look at this sign which has just come on at Ulm station. It tells you details about the next train due to arrive. Answer the questions below. (Answers p. 132)

a. What platform is it? ....

b. What's the train's final destination? ....

c. Where does it stop first? ....

d. When is the train due to leave? ....

e. Do you have to pay an Intercity surcharge? ....

2 This is an excerpt of the timetable at Ulm station. Study it, then answer the questions below. (Answers p. 132)

Zeit	Zug	Richtung	Gleis
19.42	D 411 ⬛ ⚑ ▼	Rosenheim 22.20 - Salzburg 23.22 - Villach Westbf 3.06 - Zagreb 8.16 - Skopje 22.11 - Athènes 14.35 Platzkartenpflichtig für Reisende nach dem Ausland; Für den innerdeutschen Verkehr nicht zugelassen, ausgenommen Reisende nach Rosenheim.	**2**
19.42	D 898 ⬛ ▼	Stuttgart 20.52 - Heidelberg 22.31 - Darm- stadt 23.09 - Frankfurt (M) 23.37 - Kassel 2.54 - Kreiensen 4.29 - Hannover 5.48 - Hamburg- Altona 8.37 - Kiel 9.57 mit Halt in Geislingen, Göppingen, Plochingen 🚌 Wilhelmshaven 9.45, an ⑦ 🚌 Bremerhaven-Lehe 8.58, auch 12. IV., nicht 11. IV.	**3**
⌷ **19.55** außer ⑥ nicht 24. bis 26. XII., 31. XII. bis 2. I., 9. bis 11. IV.	⬛519 ✗	Augsburg 20.38 - München 21.13	**2**
19.59	⬛594 ✗	Stuttgart 20.57 - Mannheim 22.27 - (⬛ 570 Frankfurt (M) 23.17) Kaiserslautern 23.17 - Saarbrücken 23.58	**1**

a. If you wanted to go to Stuttgart by Intercity, which train would you take and which platform would you leave from? ....

b. Do you have to pay an Intercity supplement if you wanted to go to Frankfurt at about twenty to eight? ....

c. If you were heading for Greece, at what time would you leave and from which platform? ....

d. Can you go to Munich at around 8 p.m.? ....

Did you know?

Travelling by rail

The railway in West Germany is operated by the **Deutsche Bundesbahn** (DB). If you want to get quickly from one place to another, use either the **Intercity** (first and second class) or **TEE**-trains (first class only). Otherwise you can use a **Schnellzug** or an **Eilzug** (both fairly fast) or a **Nahverkehrszug** (local train) if you wanted to stop at a smaller place.

It is about twice as expensive to travel first class as it is second class, and there is a special surcharge on **Intercity** trains for both first and second class. However, there are many special reductions (see note p. 121), and in general rail travel is cheaper in the Federal Republic than in the U.S.

If you feel like cycling, you can rent a bicycle at one of about 100 stations, together with a map of specially recommended routes for cycling.

Travelling by air

Major cities will offer domestic and international services. There is usually a bus operating between the airport and the city centre and the main train station. There are often special deals for tourists, and inside Germany flights on weekends are about one third cheaper. Lufthansa and British Airways offer a cheap weekend rate between major German and British airports.

Travelling by car

Foreigners may drive their cars in Germany for up to one year if they hold a national or international driving licence (national for citizens of EEC countries). Don't forget your registration documents and – if you want fully comprehensive insurance coverage – your international insurance certificate (green card). There is no speed limit on motorways in Germany. Within towns it is 50 km (31 m/ph), and 100 km (62 m/ph) on open roads. As you will know, traffic drives on the right. Important: unless otherwise regulated whoever comes from the right has priority.

Most gas stations (**Tankstellen**) have self-service facilities. If not, ask the attendant to fill your tank up and say **volltanken bitte!** Or, if you want a specific amount, say for example **10 Liter bitte!** (3.78 litres = 1 gallon; 1 km = 5/8 of a mile)

Your turn to speak

1 Imagine you're buying a ticket to Hamburg. You'll practice:

Einfach bitte
Wann fährt. . .?
Von welchem Gleis?

2 You're at a travel agent (**Reisebüro**) enquiring about fares to Basle (**Basel**). You'll practice:

Wie komme ich am besten. . .
Am Wochenende
Dann nehme ich lieber. . .

Revision/Review please turn to p. 219

Answers

Practice what you have learned p. 126 Exercise 1(a) 1 (b) an Intercity train (c) yes (d) see route in margin

p. 127 Exercise 2(b) Eilzug nach Frankfurt, Abfahrt 11.22 Uhr Gleis 7 (c) Schnellzug nach München, Abfahrt 11.34 Uhr Gleis 2

p. 127 Exercise 3(a) München (b) Intercity (c) Zug (d) Gleis

p. 128 Exercise 4 You should have filled in the form like this:
Ulm ab **22.01,**
Donauwörth an **22.59,**
Donauwörth ab **23.26,**
Berlin-Zoo an **7.30**

Preis: 152,58 DM für eine Fahrkarte zweiter Klasse nach Berlin Zoo.
Liegewagen: zirka 18 DM, **Schlafwagen:** zirka 40 DM

p. 128 Exercise 5(a) F (b) F (c) R (d) R (e) F (f) R

Read and understand p. 130 Exercise 1(a) 2 (b) Berchtesgaden (c) München (d) 10.55 (e) yes

p. 130 Exercise 2(a) 19:59, platform 1 (b) no (c) 19:42, platform 2 (d) yes – at 19:56

10 Ordering a meal

What you will learn

- to ask for information on different types of restaurants
- to ask about local specialties
- to order the special dish of the day
- to choose wine

and you will read about national specialties, meal times and different wines.

Restaurant am Münsterplatz

Eine Stätte gepflegter heimischer Gastlichkeit

- Gut geführte Küche mit Spezialitäten
- Ausgezeichnete Weine
- Dortmunder Union-Biere und
- Schlösser Alt vom Faß

Zum Roten Eber

Before you begin

Have a look again at Unit 4 where you have learned how to ask for a table, the menu, the bill and how to order drinks and snacks.

Study guide

	Dialogues 1, 2: listen straight through without the book
	Dialogues 1, 2: listen, read and study notes
	Dialogues 3, 4: listen straight through without the book
	Dialogues 3, 4: listen, read and study one by one
	Dialogues 5, 6: listen straight through without the book
	Dialogues 5, 6: listen, read and study notes
	Study the *Key words and phrases*
	Do the exercises in *Practice what you have learned*
	Read the *Grammar* section and do the exercise
	Do the exercise in *Read and understand*
	Read *Did you know?*
	Do the exercises in *Your turn to speak*
	Listen to all the dialogues once again straight through

Dialogues

1 *In the street. Where is there a good place to eat?*

Ruth Entschuldigen Sie, wo kann man hier gut essen?
Mann Am besten hinterm Rathaus. Da hat's mehrere Wirtschaften, und da können Sie sehr gut essen.
Ruth Was gibt es denn da?
Mann Ja, spezielle schwäbische Gerichte, aber auch Hausmannskost.

die Hausmannskost home cooking

2 *At the tourist office*

Ruth Wo kann man hier gut essen?
Frau Oswald Es gibt verschiedene Lokale, wo man gut essen kann. Ich will vielleicht eins nennen: die Forelle. Es gibt dort Fischspezialitäten und vor allem auch schwäbische Spezialitäten, wie Zwiebelrostbraten mit Spätzle zum Beispiel.

die Forelle the Trout (a popular name for restaurants)
vor allem above all
♦ **zum Beispiel** (abbreviated to z.B.) for example.

3 *Are there any places where you can have a cheap meal?*

Ruth Und wo kann man hier billig essen?
Frau Oswald Also sehr günstig und zwar mit Selbstbedienung das McDonald. Das gibt es ja überall in Europa, und das ist in der Nähe vom Hauptbahnhof.

günstig reasonable
♦ **mit Selbstbedienung** with self service
überall everywhere
♦ **Europa** Europe

1 ♦ **wo kann man hier gut essen?** where can you eat well here? Similarly:
wo kann man hier billig essen? where can you eat cheaply? (see Dialogue 3),
wo kann man hier schnell essen? where can you get a quick meal?
wo kann man hier spanisch essen? where can you get Spanish food?

hinterm Rathaus (short for **hinter dem Rathaus**) behind the town hall.

da hat's mehrere Wirtschaften there are several inns there. **Da hat's**
(= **hat es**) is a South German way of saying **da gibt es** (= there are).

♦ **was gibt es denn da?** what is there (to eat?) See *Grammar* section for more
details on **es gibt.**

♦ **spezielle schwäbische Gerichte** special Swabian dishes.

2 ♦ **verschiedene Lokale** various restaurants; **das Lokal** = pub, restaurant; see
also **das Speiselokal** = eating house, **das Tanzlokal** = dance hall.

ich will vielleicht eins nennen I want perhaps to mention one. (**nennen** =
to mention, to name).

♦ **Fischspezialitäten** fish specialties; **die Spezialität** = specialty.

Zwiebelrostbraten mit Spätzle beef roast with onions and **Spätzle** (a type
of pasta popular in Swabia).

3 ♦ **in der Nähe vom Hauptbahnhof** near the main train station (lit. in the
neighborhood of the main train station). Similarly: **in der Nähe vom
Restaurant** (near the restaurant), **in der Nähe vom Rathaus** (near the
town hall).

The 'Forelle' restaurant in Ulm

4 *Any local specialties?*

Ruth Gibt es auch Ulmer Spezialitäten?
Herr Schmid Ja, Ulm ist ja bekannt für seine Spätzle, eine handgemachte Mehlspeise, und dann gibt es zum Mittagessen auch noch die Maultaschen.
Ruth Und zum Trinken?
Herr Schmid Ja, da ist das Ulmer Bier ganz berühmt. Wir haben zwei große Ulmer Brauereien.

ganz berühmt very famous
die Brauerei brewery

5 *In the restaurant. What's today's special?*

Ruth Was ist die Spezialität des Tages?
Fräulein Serbisches Reisfleisch und Kopfsalat.
Ruth Aha. Und was kostet das?
Fräulein Sechs Mark neunzig.

6 *Choosing a wine. Which one can be recommended?*

Ruth Ich hätte gerne einen Wein bitte. Was können Sie mir da empfehlen?
Fräulein Ja, Rot- oder Weißwein, oder Weißherbst?
Ja, da haben wir einmal den Kröver Nacktarsch, der ist sehr süß, ist ein Moselwein. Und dann haben wir den Ihringer Vulkanfelsen, das ist auch ein süßlicher Wein. Die anderen sind alles Württemberger Weine, und die Württemberger sind sehr herb.

♦ **süßlich** sweetish
♦ **herb** dry (of wines)
die anderen the others

4 ◆ **bekannt für seine Spätzle** famous for its Spätzle.

eine handgemachte Mehlspeise a homemade pastry (lit. a handmade flour dish).

◆ **zum Mittagessen** for lunch; **das Mittagessen** = lunch. Similarly: **zum Frühstück** (for breakfast), **zum Abendessen** (for supper).

Maultaschen a kind of ravioli.

zum Trinken to drink. You can also say **zu trinken**.

5 **serbisches Reisfleisch** a Serbian meat and rice dish. (**der Reis** = rice, **das Fleisch** = meat).

der Kopfsalat lettuce, usually dressed with vinaigrette.

◆ **Spezialität des Tages** today's special. Similarly: **die Spezialität des Hauses** (specialty of the house).

6 ◆ **ich hätte gerne** I would like (instead of **ich möchte gerne**).

Weißherbst name of a local rosé wine (lit. white autumn). Usually rosé wines are called **Rosé-Weine**.

◆ **was können Sie mir da empfehlen?** what do you recommend me? (lit. what can you recommend me?)

◆ **der Moselwein** Moselle wine. Like the Rhine, the river Moselle has many vineyards on its banks.

Kröver Nacktarsch, Ihringer Vulkanfelsen names of white wines.

◆ **Württemberger Weine** wines from **Württemberg**. **Württemberg** is part of the South German federal state **Baden-Württemberg**. There are also wines from **Baden (Badische Weine)** (see p. 145).

Key words and phrases

To use

Wo kann man hier. . .	Where can you get. . .
gut	good
billig	cheap
schnell	fast
italienisch	Italian
spanisch	Spanish
griechisch . . . essen?	Greek . . . food?

Wo ist hier ein Lokal/Speiselokal?	Where is there a pub/restaurant?

Was gibt es. . .	What is there. . .
zum Mittagessen?	for lunch?
zum Abendessen?	for supper?
zu trinken?	to drink?

Was gibt es denn da?	What is there (to eat?)
Gibt es auch. . .?	Is/are there also. . .?
Was ist die Spezialität. . .	What is the specialty of . . .
des Tages?	the day?
des Hauses?	the house?

Was können Sie mir empfehlen?	What do you recommend me?
Ich hätte gerne. . .	I would like. . .

To understand

Das ist (ein Restaurant) mit Selbstbedienung	That's (a restaurant) with self-service
In der Nähe vom Hauptbahnhof	Near the main train station
Da gibt es schwäbische Gerichte	There are Swabian dishes
Ulm ist bekannt für seine Spezialitäten	Ulm is famous for its specialties
Wir haben (zum Beispiel). . .	We have (for example). . .
Moselweine	Moselle wines
Württemberger Weine	Württemberg wines
Der Wein ist süß/herb	This wine is sweet/dry

Practice what you have learned

1 Someone is looking for a good place to eat. Listen to the cassette a few times, then answer the questions below. (Answers p. 146)

New vocabulary
zum Lamm the lamb (lit. to the lamb), a popular name for pubs and restaurants. Similarly **zum Bären** the bear, **zum Ochsen** the ox, **zum Adler** the eagle

a. What type of food is the young man looking for?

  ☐ German specialties

  ☐ Greek food

  ☐ Spanish food

b. Is the restaurant 'zum Lamm'

  ☐ good but expensive?

  ☐ good and good value for the money?

c. Is the restaurant

  ☐ far away?

  ☐ quite near by?

Ältester Gasthof Deutschlands

Zum Roten Bären

Erbaut um 1120

2 A young man orders food and drink in a restaurant. Listen to the dialogue, then tick the right boxes below. (Answers p. 146)

New vocabulary
Salzkartoffeln potatoes boiled in salt water, then coated with butter

a. What is the specialty of the day?

  ☐ fish

  ☐ a roast

  ☐ chicken

b. What does the guest choose?

  ☐ chicken

  ☐ fish

c. What is served with the dish he chooses?

  ☐ potatoes and salad

  ☐ Spätzle

d. What kind of wine does he want? (Tick two boxes)

  ☐ white

  ☐ red

  ☐ sweet

  ☐ dry

e. Which wine does he choose in the end?

  ☐ a Württemberg wine

  ☐ a Moselle wine

3 A customer is paying for food for 3 people at a self-service restaurant.
What's on his tray? Study the menu below, then listen to the cashier and
pick out the items she rings up on the register. Write the items and their
prices in the spaces below and add them up. (Answers p. 146)

New vocabulary
das Schweineschnitzel slice of pork
die Schweinshaxe pig's knuckles
das Schweinskotelett pork cutlet

a. .... **DM** ....

b. .... **DM** ....

c. .... **DM** ....

(total) **DM** ....

4 You'll hear a woman ordering food from the menu below. Can you write down the items she orders and make out the bill (**die Rechnung**) (Answers p. 146)

New vocabulary
das Hauptgericht main dish   **das Kalbsfilet** veal filet
das Brathähnchen roast chicken   **die Beilage** side dish

```
                    S p e i s e k a r t e
                         SUPPEN

Tagessuppe ...............................................DM   1.50
Tomatensuppe .............................................DM   1.20


                       HAUPTGERICHTE

1/2 Brathähnchen mit Pommes Frites ......................DM   6.30
Kalbsfilet mit Reis oder Butterkartoffeln................DM  13.50
Rostbraten mit Spätzle...................................DM   8.90
Rumpsteak mit Pommes Frites..............................DM  12.80


                         BEILAGEN

Frisches Gemüse..........................................DM   1.50
Gemischter Salat.........................................DM   1.70
```

RECHNUNG a. .... **DM** ....

           b. .... **DM** ....

           c. .... **DM** ....

                                                      DM ....

5 A dissatisfied customer. Listen to the tape. What is she complaining about? (Answers p. 146)

New vocabulary
salzig salty
scharf hot
bitter bitter

a. The soup is too ....

d. The wine is too ....

b. The meat is too ....

e. The cake is too ....

c. The sauce is too ....

f. The coffee is too ....

Grammar

Expressing 'there is' and 'there are'

In German there is only one way of saying *both* 'there is' (singular) and 'there are' (plural): **es gibt**.

Singular

Es gibt ein Theater in Ulm.	There's a theatre in Ulm.
Gibt es hier eine Bank?	Is there a bank here?

Plural

Es gibt verschiedene Lokale, wo man gut essen kann.	There are several restaurants where you can eat well.
Gibt es Brauereien in Ulm?	Are there breweries in Ulm?

Often you will find **es gibt** followed by **zu** or **zum**:

Was gibt es zum Mittagessen?	What is there for lunch?
Was gibt es zum Trinken?	What is there to drink?
Es gibt nichts mehr zu essen.	There's nothing more to eat.

Note: Verbs, e.g. **essen** or **trinken**, are spelled with a small letter after **zu** and a large one after **zum**. Stick to **zu** yourself – it's easier.

Sometimes **es gibt** cannot be neatly translated by 'there is' or 'there are', e.g.

Das gibt es nicht.	That doesn't exist.
Das gibt es überall in Europa.	You'll find it everywhere in Europe.
Wo gibt es denn sowas?	Would you believe it!

Exercise Translate into German. (Answers p. 146)

a. What is there for lunch? ....

....

b. What is there for breakfast? ....

....

c. Are there theatres in Munich? ....

....

d. There is fish, and there are Spanish specialities ....

....

e. There are potatoes and fried sausage for lunch ....

....

Read and understand

This is just a small selection of restaurants from a tourist information leaflet about Ulm. Study it and answer the questions below.
(Answers p. 146)

New vocabulary
SB=Selbstbedienung self service
für den eiligen Gast for the customer who is in a hurry
das Wild game, venison

No.	Name des Lokals	Öffnungszeiten	Ruhetag	Spezialitäten
1	**Adler**	10.00–24.00	Sonntag	Hausmannskost
2	**Bei Niko**	11.00–24.00	–	Griechische Spezialitäten
3	**Braustüble**	10.00–24.00	Montag	Schwäbische und spanische Spezialitäten
4	**Fischhaus Heilbronner**	9.00–18.00	Sonntag	Fisch und Wild
5	**McDonalds**	9.00–23.00	–	Big Mäc
6	**Hertie SB Restaurant**	10.30–18.30	Sonntag	für den eiligen Gast
7	**Schlössle**	10.00–24.00	Sonntag	Schweizer Spezialitäten

a. Where would you go if you felt like a quick snack, but did not want to eat a hamburger?

....

b. Where would you go for Greek food?

....

c. If you wanted home cooking where would you go?

....

d. If you were looking for Swiss dishes?

....

e. Can you get Spanish specialties on a Monday?

....

f. Can you get venison after 6 p.m.?

....

Did you know?

More about food

It's not all **Bratwurst, Sauerkraut, Kartoffeln** and **Bier** – nowadays German
cuisine is much more sophisticated. There aren't any national specialities as
such, but a great many regional dishes, and the foreign influence has
increased over the past twenty years. This is mainly due to the arrival of the
Turkish, Greek, Italian, Yugoslav and Spanish guest workers in the Federal
Republic who have brought their cuisine – and restaurants – with them.
German dishes still tend to be very rich and almost invariably meat-based,
but there is also an increasing trend towards **leichte Kost** (light diet) –
especially among younger people who are very health and figure conscious.

The regional and local specialities are too numerous to be mentioned
here. The best thing is to try them out – just ask for **Spezialitäten**.

Meal times

In Germany the main meal of the day is lunch, served around one o'clock.
If possible, the Germans stick to their hot **Mittagessen** even at work (many
firms provide cafeterias. The evening meal (**Abendessen** or **Abendbrot**) is
around seven p.m. and usually consists of slices of cold meat, sausage or
cheese on bread. Sometimes a soup or a salad is served, but in general there
is no cooked food. Guests are often invited on Sundays for coffee and cakes
– **Kaffee und Kuchen** – around four o'clock in the afternoon. At
restaurants, of course, you can get a hot meal till late in the evening.

Wines

Best known are **Rheinwein** (wines from the Rhine area, the most
famous being **Liebfraumilch**) and **Moselwein** (wines from the
Moselle). Both wines are rather sweet; **Moselwein** has a lighter and
fruitier taste. Other well-known German wines are grown on the
banks of the rivers **Nahe, Saar** and **Ruwer** (all tributaries to the
Rhine). And if you go to Germany, it is well worth trying
Frankenwein (from Franconia, an area south of Frankfurt) as well as
the **Württemberger** and **Badische Weine**. All these wines are drier
than the Rhine or Moselle wines, and often very aromatic. Most of
the German wines are white; there are only very few red ones.
Austria and Switzerland are also wine-producing countries.

*Vineyards
on the
Rhine*

Your turn to speak

1 You want to find out where you can eat well, cheaply, and quickly. Repeat the questions in German after Michael's prompt on the cassette. You'll practice:

Wo kann man hier . . . essen?

2 First study the menu below. On tape you'll be asked to order several items from this menu according to Michael's prompts. Make sure you understand the menu, and read it aloud before you do the exercise.

SUPPEN

Bouillion mit Ei
Tomatensuppe
Kartoffelsuppe

HAUPTGERICHTE

½ Brathähnchen
   mit Kartoffelsalat
Rindsbraten mit Zwiebeln
Schweineschnitzel mit grünem
   Gemüse
Forelle blau mit Salatplatte

BEILAGEN

Reis
Nudeln
Salzkartoffeln
Pommes frites
Gemischter Salat

WEINE

weiß Ihringer Vulkanfels (süßlich)
    Alter Salzberg (herb)
rot Sonnenberger Trollinger (herb)

Answers

Practice what you have learned, p. 139 Exercise 1(a) German specialties (b) good and good value for the money (c) quite near by

p. 139 Exercise 2(a) a roast (b) fish (c) potatoes and salad (d) white, dry (e) a Württemberg wine

p. 140 Exercise 3(a) Schweineschnitzel mit Pommes Frites DM 6,50 (b) Schweinshaxe mit Salatplatte DM 4,90 (c) Kartoffelsalat DM 1,30; altogether 12,70 DM

p. 141 Exercise 4(a) Tomatensuppe DM 1,20 (b) Rumpsteak mit Pommes Frites DM 12,80 (c) Beilage: Gemischter Salat DM 1,70; altogether 15,70

p. 142 Exercise 5(a) salty (b) hard (c) hot (d) dry (e) sweet (f) bitter

Grammar p. 143 (a) Was gibt es zum Mittagessen? (b) Was gibt es zum Frühstück? (c) Gibt es Theater in München? (d) Es gibt Fisch, und es gibt spanische Spezialitäten. (e) Es gibt Kartoffeln und Bratwurst zum Mittagessen.

Read and understand, p. 144 (a) to the **Hertie SB Restaurant** (b) to **Bei Niko** (c) to the **Adler** (d) to the **Schlössle** (e) no (f) no

11 Likes and dislikes

What you will learn

- to say whether you like or dislike something, such as a particular town or region, your job, or food
- to say what you enjoy doing

and you will be reading about the different attractions of particular regions in Germany.

Study guide

	Dialogues 1, 2 listen straight through without the book
	Dialogues 1, 2 listen, read and study one by one
	Dialogues 3, 4 listen without the book
	Dialogues 3, 4 listen, read and study one by one
	Dialogue 5 listen without the book
	Dialogue 5 listen, read and study notes
	Study the *Key words and phrases*
	Do the exercises in *Practice what you have learned*
	Read the *Grammar* section
	Do the exercise in *Read and understand*
	Read *Did you know?*
	Do the exercises in *Your turn to speak*
	Listen to all the dialogues once again straight through

Dialogues

1 *How do Hussein and Eliot like it in Ulm?*

Ruth Wie gefällt es dir hier?
Hussein Gut.
Ruth Gefällt dir die Schule?
Hussein Ja.

Ruth Wie gefällt dir's hier?
Eliot Prima.
Ruth Was gefällt dir besonders?
Eliot Ah, meine Freunde.

prima excellent, first class
♦ **Freunde** pl. (sing. **der Freund**) friends

2 *Does Frau Klein like it in Ulm?*

Ruth Gefällt es Ihnen in Ulm?
Frau Klein Ja, es gefällt mir gut.
Ruth Was gefällt Ihnen denn vor allen Dingen?
Frau Klein Also die Altstadt, und an der Donau kann man schön spazieren
gehen, und die Leute sind auch ziemlich freundlich, und die
Geschäfte . . .

vor allen Dingen above all things
die Altstadt old part of town
♦ **die Leute** the people
♦ **freundlich** friendly

1 ◆ **wie gefällt es dir hier?** how do you like it here? (lit. how pleases it to you here?) This is a very common phrase and comes from the verb **gefallen** (to please). **Dir** means 'to you' when talking to children.

gefällt dir die Schule? do you like school?

wie gefällt dir's hier? Ruth made a mistake here. She should have said **wie gefällt's dir hier** which is short for **wie gefällt es dir hier.**

◆ **was gefällt dir besonders?** what do you like especially?

2 ◆ **gefällt es Ihnen in Ulm?** do you like it in Ulm? **Ihnen** means 'to you' when you are talking to adults.

◆ **ja, es gefällt mir gut** yes, I like it a lot. If you *don't* like something you say, **nein, es gefällt mir nicht.** And if you are not sure you just say
◆ **es geht** (so-so; lit. it goes).

. . . kann man spazieren gehen you can go for walks.

3 *Does Herr Vollmert prefer North Germany to South Germany?*

Ruth   Was gefällt Ihnen besser: Norddeutschland oder Süddeutschland?

Herr Vollmert   Mmm – ich liebe beides. Schwierig zu sagen. Im Moment gefällt es mir sehr gut hier in Süddeutschland.

4 *Ruth interviews two people about food and travelling*

Ruth   Was essen Sie gern?

Herr Hansen   Fleisch in jeder Variation, am liebsten Steaks.

Ruth   Und was trinken Sie am liebsten?

Herr Hansen   Westdeutsches Bier, am liebsten Königspils.

Ruth   Reisen Sie gerne?

Junge Frau   Ja, sehr gerne.

Ruth   Wohin?

Junge Frau   Eigentlich überall hin, – eh – aber am liebsten in den Süden.

(das) Königspils brand name of a pils beer

3 ◆ **was gefällt Ihnen besser?** what do you like better? (lit. what pleases to you better?)

Norddeutschland oder Süddeutschland? North Germany or South Germany? These two parts of Germany are quite different in character and even in language.

◆ **ich liebe beides** I love both. The opposite of **lieben** (to love) is **hassen** (to hate). You should use both only when you feel very strongly about something; usually you just say **es gefällt mir** or **es gefällt mir nicht.**

schwierig zu sagen difficult to say.

4 ◆ **was essen Sie gern?** what do you like eating? Remember that **gern** (or **gerne**) is always used to emphasize liking, e.g. **ich möchte gerne** (I'd very much like), **was hätten Sie gerne?** (what would you like?) And if you want to express that you like something best you say **am liebsten**, e.g.

◆ **am liebsten Steaks** steaks best. Similarly: **ich esse am liebsten Fisch** (I like fish best), **ich trinke am liebsten Bier** (I like beer best.) And if you want to say that you prefer something you say

◆ **lieber**, e.g. **ich esse lieber Fisch** (I like fish better), **ich trinke lieber Wein** (I like wine better).

Fleisch in jeder Variation meat of all kind.

westdeutsches Bier beer from the western region of Germany. Note that citizens of the Federal Republic say **westdeutsch** and **Westdeutschland** when referring to the western parts of the republic, and not to 'West Germany' i.e. as opposed to 'East Germany'.

eigentlich überall hin everywhere really. The word **hin** is often added to statements. It carries the idea of 'away', 'towards'.

◆ **reisen Sie gerne?** do you like travelling?

in den Süden to the South (e.g. Mediterranean countries). Here it is **in den Süden** (accusative) and not **im** (= **in dem**) (dative) because you are *moving towards* a destination. See *Grammar summary* on p. 225 for more details.

5 *At the tourist office. Where do the Germans like to travel for their holidays?*

Ruth	Frau Hildenstein?
Frau Hildenstein	Ja?
Ruth	Wohin fahren die Deutschen am liebsten im Urlaub?
Frau Hildenstein	Im Sommer in den Süden, weil sie auf besseres Wetter hoffen, nach Italien, zum Teil an die Adria, oder an die Riviera, und nach Jugoslawien. Sehr beliebt jedes Jahr ist Griechenland, vor allem die griechischen Inseln.
Ruth	Und im Inland?
Frau Hildenstein	Im Inland ist an sich sehr beliebt der Bayerische Wald, oder Oberbayern, der Schwarzwald hier im Süden, oder natürlich die Nord- und Ostsee.

die Riviera the (French) Riviera
Jugoslawien Jugoslavia
sehr beliebt very popular
jedes Jahr each year
Griechenland Greece
die griechischen Inseln the Greek islands
an sich actually
der Bayerische Wald the Bavarian Forest
Oberbayern Upper Bavaria
der Schwarzwald the Black Forest
die Nord- und Ostsee the North Sea and the Baltic Sea

im Urlaub on (their) holidays.

weil sie auf besseres Wetter hoffen because they hope for better weather. Note the word order after **weil** (because): the verb (**hoffen** = to hope) goes to the *end* of the sentence.

zum Teil an die Adria partly to the Adriatic coast.

♦ **im Inland** within Germany. The opposite would be **im Ausland** (abroad or outside Germany).

Key words and phrases

die Leute	people
die Freunde	friends
freundlich	friendly
im Inland	at home
im Ausland	abroad
sehr beliebt	very popular

Mainly to understand

Wie gefällt es dir/Ihnen . . .	How do you like it . . .
hier?	here?
in Ulm?	in Ulm?
Was gefällt dir/Ihnen besonders?	What do you like especially?
Was gefällt dir/Ihnen besser?	What do you like better?
Was essen/trinken Sie . . .	What do you like eating/drinking . .
gern?	a lot?
lieber?	better?
am liebsten?	best?
Reisen Sie gern?	Do you like travelling?

To use yourself

(Ja) es gefällt mir (gut)	(Yes) I like it (a lot)
(Nein) es gefällt mir nicht (gut)	(No) I don't like it (much)
Ich liebe/hasse es	I love/hate it
Es geht	So-so
Ich esse gern/am liebsten Steaks	I like eating steaks a lot/best
Ich trinke lieber Wein	I prefer (drinking) wine
Ich reise am liebsten in den Süden	I like (travelling to) the South best

Practice what you have learned

1 Herr Marks talks about his likes and dislikes. Listen to him on the cassette. Then tick the right boxes below. (Answers p. 160)

New vocabulary
vermissen to miss
manchmal sometimes

a. Does Herr Marks like his work?

☐ yes

☐ sometimes

b. Does he miss England?

☐ no

☐ sometimes

c. He likes Munich because . . . (tick two boxes)

☐ there are so many theatres and concerts

☐ there are many shops and restaurants

☐ there are many lakes and mountains near by

2 Ruth goes to an exhibiton of modern paintings and asks an elderly gentleman and a young girl for their opinion. Listen to the conversation a few times, then answer the questions below with True or False (**Richtig oder Falsch**). (Answers p. 160)

New vocabulary
die Ausstellung exhibition
für Jugendliche for young people
alter Knabe old fellow
kräftige Farben bright colours

a. The old gentleman thinks it's probably interesting for young people, but it's not what he likes for himself. ☐R ☐F

b. He thinks it's interesting for both old and young people. ☐R ☐F

c. The young girl finds it all very interesting, but she dislikes the colours of the paintings. ☐R ☐F

d. She thinks the exhibition is quite interesting, and she likes the bright colours. ☐R ☐F

3 Ruth asks Frau Hildenstein at the tourist office where the Germans like to go for their winter holidays. Listen to the dialogue, study the map, then write down the names of the popular regions in the order in which they're mentioned. (Answers p. 160)

New vocabulary
das Skigebiet skiing area

a. ....

b. ....

c. ....

d. ....

4 Match up the questions and answers below first, then listen to the cassette to check.

a. Gefällt es Ihnen in Ulm? ....

b. Was gefällt Ihnen besser, Norddeutschland oder Süddeutschland?

   ....

c. Reisen Sie gern? ....

d. Und wohin reisen Sie am liebsten? ....

e. Was essen Sie gern? ....

f. Und was trinken Sie am liebsten? ....

Ja, sehr gern   Am liebsten in den Süden   Am liebsten Moselwein

Chinesische Gerichte

Süddeutschland   Ja, es gefällt mir gut

Grammar

The use of 'gefallen'

You use the verb **gefallen** if you want to say that you like something. The most important forms of **gefallen** are used in phrases like these:

Gefällt es Ihnen?	Do you like it? (lit. pleases it to you?)
Wie gefällt es Ihnen hier?	How do you like it here? (lit. how pleases it to you here?)
Gefällt dir die Schule?	Do you like school?
Was gefällt dir besonders?	What do you like especially?
Was gefällt dir besser?	What do you like better?

Note: Both **Ihnen** and **dir** mean 'to you'. You use **Ihnen** with adults and **dir** with children and friends.

If you want to say that *you* like something, you use **gefallen** + **mir**, e.g.

Es gefällt mir hier.	I like it here.
Ulm gefällt mir.	I like Ulm.
Die Stadt gefällt mir gut.	I like the town a lot.
Norddeutschland gefällt mir besser.	I like North Germany better.

And if you don't like something you just add **nicht**, e.g.

Es gefällt mir hier nicht.	I don't like it here.
Ulm gefällt mir nicht.	I don't like Ulm.
Die Stadt gefällt mir nicht.	I don't like the town.

The use of 'gern, lieber, am liebsten'

Another way of saying you like something, is to use **gern**, e.g.

Ich esse gern Steaks.	I like eating steaks.
Ich trinke gern Kaffee.	I like drinking coffee.
Ich fahre gern in den Süden.	I like going to the South.

If you *prefer* something, or if you would rather do something else, you use **lieber**, e.g.

Ich möchte lieber Wein.	I'd rather have wine.
Ich esse lieber Fisch.	I prefer eating fish.
Ich nehme lieber den Zug.	I'd rather take the train.

And if you like something *best*, you use **am liebsten**, e.g.

Ich esse am liebsten Fleisch.	I like eating meat best.
Ich reise am liebsten nach England.	I like going to England best.
Ich möchte am liebsten Kuchen.	I'd like some cake most of all.

Read and understand

Lore has written a postcard from her holiday town of Berchtesgaden. Read the postcard, then answer the questions below. (Answers p. 160)

New vocabulary

viele Grüße many greetings
könnte could
damit so that

dick fat
werden to become
schlafen to sleep

Berchtesgaden, 12. August

Liebe Hilde,
viele grüße aus Berchtesgaden.
Ein wunderschöner Urlaub!! Das
Hotel ist sehr gut, das Essen
könnte nicht besser sein! Ich gehe
viel spazieren, damit ich nicht
zu dick werde. Am liebsten liege
ich in der Sonne und schlafe!
Deine Lore

a. What is the hotel like? ....
b. Could the food be better? ....
c. What does Lore do in order to avoid putting on weight?

....

d. What is her favourite pastime? ....

Did you know?

Some popular holiday areas in Germany

1 *The North Sea* **die Nordsee**
Famous for its bracing climate, much recommended by doctors. The most popular resorts are on the East Frisian and North Frisian Islands (**ostfriesische und nordfriesische Inseln**); most famous and fashionable is the island of **Sylt**, close to the Danish border.

2 *The Baltic Sea* **die Ostsee**
The climate is milder, the seas and dunes less spectacular than those of the North Sea. There are a number of well-established seaside resorts such as Warnemünde, Kühlungsborn, Ahrenshoop and Binz. One can also come across rather futuristic resorts like Damp 2000.

3 *The Lüneburg Heath* **die Lüneburger Heide**
A stretch of beautiful health and moorland between Hamburg and Hannover. One of the few areas with a significant number of sheep in Germany. **Celle** and **Lüneburg** are the most famous towns with beautiful historic centres.

4 *The Mecklenburg Lakes* **die Mecklenburgische Seenplatte**
A vast area of hilly woodland with numerous lakes to cater for a wide range of recreation activities.

5 *The Spree Forest* **die Spreewald** (near Berlin)
A maze of waterways, dykes, weirs and small islands, ideal for boating and hiking.

6 *The Harz Mountains* **der Harz**
A wooded range of mountains popular for hiking in summer and skiing in winter. Its highest peak, the **Brocken,** is the setting for the famous Walpurgis night (**Walpurgisnacht**) in Goethe's drama *Faust.*

7 *The Eifel Mountains and the Moselle Valley* **die Eifel und das Moseltal**
The Eifel, a hilly area close to the Belgian and Luxembourg borders, is one of the oldest and most interesting landscapes in Germany. Famous are its lakes (**Maare**) in volcanic craters. The climate and scenery are rather rugged. The Moselle Valley south of the Eifel Mountains is more romantic, with steep vineyards stretching down to the meandering Moselle river.

8 *The Erz Mountains* **das Erzgebirge**
Wild and scenic mountain range along the border to Czechoslovakia, once famous for its silver and iron ore mines. Nowadays a popular tourist area for hiking, winter sports, spas and traditional crafts.

9 *The Rhine* **der Rhein**
The Rhine is one of Europe's largest, most famous and most polluted rivers. Avoid the industrial areas on the Upper Rhine around **Karlsruhe** and **Ludwigshafen** and on the Lower Rhine north of cologne (**Köln**) — the scenic bits (mountains, vineyards, castles) are between **Bonn** and **Mainz.**

10 *The Odenwald Forest* **der Odenwald**
A large, somewhat sinister forest (the Germanic hero **Siegfried** was killed here, according to the legend). There are many nature reserves and spas.

11 *The Black Forest* **der Schwarzwald**
One of the most famous German holiday areas. It has beautiful villages and spas, clean air, a mild climate, and good hiking and skiing.

12 *Lake Constance and the Alps* **der Bodensee und die Alpen**
Lake Constance (it takes its English name from the city of **Konstanz** on its southern shore) is one of the biggest lakes in western Europe. It is surrounded by the Federal Republic, Austria and Switzerland. It is famous for its mild climate and has many resorts. The German Alps can be divided into the **Allgäu** Alps just east of Lake Constance and — further east, south of Munich — the Bavarian Alps (**Bayerische Alpen**). The highest Alpine peak in Germany is the **Zugspitze** (2963 metres).

13 *The Bavarian Forest* **der Bayerische Wald**
A large stretch of woodland, close to the border with Czechoslovakia. It has lots of well-marked hiking and cross-country skiing trails, and lots of wildlife.

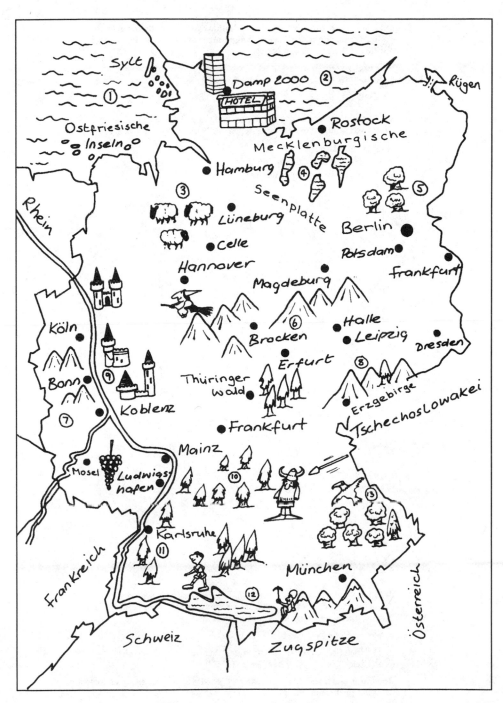

Your turn to speak

1 Imagine you're a tourist spending a holiday in the South German city of Freiburg near the Black Forest. Your tour guide wants to know whether you like it there. You'll practice:

Es gefällt mir
Sehr schön
Es geht

2 This time it's your turn to ask more questions. You're interviewing Frau Gross, who's just moved from Aachen to Munich. You'll practice:

Wie gefällt Ihnen. . .?
Was gefällt Ihnen besser?
Was gefällt Ihnen besonders?

Answers

Practice what you have learned, p. 154 Exercise **1**(a) sometimes (b) sometimes (c) because there are so many theatres and concerts, and because there are many lakes and mountains.

p. 154 Exercise **2**(a) R (b) F (c) F (d) R

p. 155 Exercise **3**(a) (Skigebiete in der) Schweiz (b) Österreich (Vorarlberg) (c) Bayerischer Wald (d) Allgäu

Read and understand, p. 157 (a) very good (b) no (c) she goes for walks (d) lying in the sun, sleeping.

12 Your town – the weather

What you will learn

- to ask for and understand information about specific towns and what they have to offer
- to talk about your hometown
- to understand some weather forecasts and make one or two comments about the weather
  and you will be given some further information about holiday areas in Austria and Switzerland.

Study guide

	Dialogue 1: listen without the book
	Dialogue 1: listen, read and study the notes
	Dialogues 2, 3: listen straight through without the book
	Dialogues 2, 3: listen, read and study one by one
	Dialogue 4: listen without the book; try to answer the question
	Dialogue 4: listen, read and study the notes
	Dialogue 5: listen several times without the book
	Dialogue 5: listen, read and study the notes
	Study the *Key words and phrases*
	Do the exercises in *Practice what you have learned*
	Read the *Grammar* section and do the exercise
	Do the exercises in *Read and understand*
	Read *Did you know?*
	Do the exercises in *Your turn to speak*
	Listen to all the dialogues once again straight through

1

At the tourist office: some sights in Freiburg

Ruth	Haben Sie Informationen über Freiburg?
Frau Hildenstein	Ja.
Ruth	Was gibt es dort alles zu sehen?
Frau Hildenstein	Zum Beispiel das Münster, dann die Musikhochschule; ein sehr schöner Rathausplatz ist dort mit dem alten und neuen Rathaus; die alte und die neue Universität, dann das Augustinermuseum. Dann kann man sehr schöne Wanderungen machen von Freiburg aus in den Schwarzwald.

- **Informationen** (pl) information
  die Musikhochschule academy of music
  new new

2

Ruth's friend Ursula asks Irene Bagehorn where she's from

Ursula	Irene, woher kommst du?
Irene	Ich komme aus Memmingen. Das ist zirka 50 Kilometer von Ulm.
Ursula	Ist das ein Dorf?
Irene	Nein, das ist kein Dorf. Es ist größer als ein Dorf. Memmingen ist eine Kleinstadt.
Ursula	Und gefällt es dir dort, oder möchtest du lieber in einer Großstadt wohnen?
Irene	Nein, mir gefällt es sehr gut dort. Ich möchte nicht in einer Großstadt wohnen. Es ist viel intimer in einer Kleinstadt, man kennt mehr Leute, es ist ruhiger, und nicht so hektisch.

- **das Dorf** village
- **die Kleinstadt** small provincial town
- **die Großstadt** big city
  intim intimate
- **ruhig** quiet
- **hektisch** hectic

The 'Freiburger Münster' ♦

1 ◆ **was gibt es dort (alles) zu sehen?** what is there to see there? **Alles** (=all) ist just a filler.

das Münster the cathedral. The **Freiburger Münster** is a very famous Gothic cathedral, dating back to the 13th century.

der Rathausplatz the town hall square. The **Rathaus** (town hall) gets its name from the verb **raten** (to advise).

das Augustinermuseum museum founded by the Augustine monks.

◆ **dann kann man sehr schöne Wanderungen machen** then you can go on very beautiful hiking tours (**die Wanderung** = hiking tour; **wandern** = to hike, to ramble).

2 ◆ **es ist größer als ein Dorf** it is bigger than a village. You use **als** (= than) for comparisons, e.g. **London ist größer als München** (London is bigger than Munich), **Ulm ist kleiner als Köln** (Ulm is smaller than Cologne). See *Grammar* section for more examples.

es ist viel intimer in einer Kleinstadt it is much more intimate in a small town. It is obvious that she is comparing the small town to a bigger one, so she doesn't have to add . . . **als in einer Großstadt** (than in a big city).

◆ **man kennt mehr Leute** you know more people.

3 *What's life like in Memmingen?*

Ursula   Und was machst du so am Abend? Nach der Arbeit?
Irene   Ja, es ist natürlich nicht viel los in Memmingen. Es gibt ein
kleines Theater, es gibt ein paar Kneipen. . . . Aber ich habe
gute Freunde, und wir unternehmen oft was zusammen.
Ursula   Was zum Beispiel?
Irene   Im Sommer machen wir Ausflüge, oder gehen zum Baden, im
Winter fahren wir Ski. Und ab und zu gibt es auch mal eine Party
Und jede Woche treffen wir uns einmal zum Kegeln.
Ursula   Kegeln? Das ist so ähnlich wie Bowling, nicht wahr?
Irene   Ja. Das macht aber sehr viel Spaß. Und nach dem Kegeln gehen
wir dann noch ein Bier trinken – manchmal auch mehr. Meistens
bin ich vor zwei Uhr nie zu Hause.

- **unternehmen** to do, to undertake
Ausflüge (pl) (sing. **der Ausflug**) trips, excursions
das Kegeln skittles (ninepin)
meistens in most cases
nie never
- **zu Hause** at home

4 *Rainer Schilz comes from a big city in northern Germany. Can you
guess which one? You'll hear the answer on tape.*

Ursula   Herr Schilz, woher kommen Sie?
Herr Schilz   Ich komme aus einer Großstadt in Norddeutschland. Die Stadt hat
ungefähr zwei Millionen Einwohner. Sie liegt an einem Fluß – an
einem großen Fluß: an der Elbe. Sie ist bekannt für ihr
Nachtleben. Da gibt es zum Beispiel eine Straße, die heißt
Reeperbahn, mit vielen Bars, Klubs, Diskotheken, und so weiter.
Mir gefällt es in der Stadt. Die Atmosphäre ist immer liberal und
tolerant.

- **das Nachtleben** nightlife
die Bar bar
der Klub club
die Diskothek discothèque
die Atmosphäre atmosphere
liberal liberal
tolerant tolerant

3 ◆ **es ist nicht viel los** there's nothing much going on. The opposite would be
◆ **es ist immer etwas los** there's always something going on.

◆ **wir gehen zum Baden** we go bathing, or simpler, **wir gehen baden**.
Similarly: **wir gehen schwimmen** (we go swimming), **wir gehen tanzen** (we
go dancing), **wir gehen kegeln** (we go to play skittles [ninepin]).

im Winter fahren wir Ski in winter we go skiing (lit. in winter go we ski).
Skifahren (to ski) is a separable verb.

◆ **jede Woche treffen wir uns einmal** we meet once every week.

so ähnlich wie Bowling nicht wahr? similar to bowling, isn't it?

◆ **das macht sehr viel Spaß** that's a lot of fun.

◆ **ab und zu gibt es (auch mal) eine Party** every now and then there is a
party. You will have noticed by now that there are a lot of 'filler words'
(here: **auch mal**) in German. They carry no special meaning, but give the
language a certain flavour. Other popular 'filler words' are **dann, noch,
nun, doch, schon, ja, denn, aber,** etc. You won't use them yourself but it
helps if you recognise them when they're being used.

4 ◆ **zwei Millionen Einwohner** two million inhabitants.

◆ **sie liegt an einem Fluß** it is (lit. lies) beside a river. **Sie** (lit. she) refers to
the feminine noun **die Stadt**. Similarly: **sie liegt an einem See** (it lies
beside a lake), **sie liegt an einem Berg** (it lies at the foot of a mountain.)

an der Elbe by the (river) Elbe.

die Reeperbahn name of a street in the city in question.

5 *A weather report on the radio*

Die Vorhersage bis morgen abend. Südbayern und Donaugebiet
mit Bayerischem Wald: heute sonnig. Morgen nachmittag und
abend einzelne gewittrige Schauer. Höchsttemperaturen 23 bis 27
Grad, in den Alpen in 2000 Meter Höhe um 13 Grad. Schwacher
bis mäßiger Wind aus Südwest bis West.

die Vorhersage bis morgen abend the forecast till tomorrow evening. Note
that **morgen** can mean both 'tomorrow' and 'morning', e. g. **morgen abend**
(tomorrow evening), **morgen mittag** (noon tomorrow), **morgen früh** (early
tomorrow), BUT **guten Morgen** (good morning), **heute morgen** (this
morning), **gestern morgen** (yesterday morning). If **morgen** comes first it
means 'tomorrow'. Also note the capital in **guten Morgen**.

heute sonnig sunny today (**die Sonne** = the sun).

einzelne gewittrige Schauer some thundershowers (**der Schauer** =
shower, **das Gewitter** = thunderstorm).

Höchsttemperaturen 23 bis 27 Grad maximum temperatures 23 to 27
degrees centigrade. Temperature in Germany is always referred to in
centigrade (= Celsius). Conversion to Fahrenheit: multiply the centigrade
figure by 9, divide by 5, add 32, e.g. 23 to 27°C would be 73 to 81°F.

in den Alpen in 2000 Meter Höhe um 13 Grad in the Alps at 2000 metres
(of altitude), around 13 degrees.

schwacher bis mäßiger Wind aus Südwest bis West light to moderate
wind from southwest to west. Here are all the four directions: **Nord,
West, Ost, Süd** (north, west, east, south).

Weather terms

You will probably not need to use a lot of weather terms, but it is always useful to understand the weather forecast if you are travelling. Here is a list of some more terms you are likely to hear.

die Sonne the sun
heiter bright, fair
heiter bis wolkig sunny intervals
trocken dry

der Regen rain.
vereinzelt Schauer occasional showers
naß wet

Wolken (pl.) clouds
wolkig cloudy
wechselhaft changeable

der Schnee snow
das Eis ice
das Glatteis ice patch
unter Null below zero
der Frost frost

der Nebel fog
neblig foggy
Nebelfelder fog patches

Key words and phrases

Haben Sie Informationen über. . .?	Have you got (any) information about. . . ?
Was gibt es dort zu sehen?	What is there to see?
Ich komme aus. . .	I come from . . .
einer Großstadt	a big city
einer Kleinstadt	a small provincial town
einem Dorf	a village
Meine Stadt . . .	My town . . .
liegt an einem Fluß	is beside a river
ist bekannt für ihr Nachtleben	is famous for its nightlife
hat . . . Einwohner	has . . . inhabitants
Es ist größer/kleiner als . . .	It is bigger/smaller than . . .
Es ist ruhig/hektisch	It is quiet/hectic
Es ist nichts/etwas los	There is nothing/something going on
Wir unternehmen oft was zusammen	We do a lot together
Wir treffen uns jede Woche einmal	We meet once a week
Das macht viel Spaß	That's a lot of fun
Wir gehen. . .	We go . . .
baden	bathing
kegeln	to play skittles (ninepin)
tanzen	dancing
Ab und zu gibt es eine Party	Every now and then there is a party
Zu Hause	At home

See p. 167 for key words and phrases about the weather.

Practice what you have learned

1 On tape Lutz will tell you about some major sights and events in West and East Berlin. Listen carefully, then tick off those sights and events he mentions. (Answers p. 174)

Westberlin

☐ **a. Gedächtniskirche**
Memorial church

☐ **b. Schloß Charlottenburg**
Charlottenburg Palace

☐ **c. Rathaus Schöneberg**
Schöneberg town hall

☐ **d. Grüne Woche**
Agricultural week

☐ **e. Jazz-Tage**
Jazz festival

☐ **f. Film-Festival**
Film festival

☐ **g. Zoo**
Zoo

☐ **h. Grunewald**
Grunewald forest

☐ **i. Wannsee**
Lake Wannsee

Ostberlin

☐ **k. Fernsehturm**
TV tower

☐ **l. Pergamon-Museum**
Pergamon museum

☐ **m. Schloß Sanssouci**
Sanssouci Palace

2 On tape you will hear a radio advertisement inviting you to come to **Luzern** (Lucerne), a picturesque town in the heart of Switzerland. Listen a few times, then tick the right boxes below. (Answers p. 174)

New vocabulary
willkommen welcome
die Brücke bridge
die Sterne (pl) stars

der Sessellift chair lift
die Seilbahn cable car
genießen to enjoy

a. Is there an old part of town?
☐ yes
☐ no

b. Luzern is situated
☐ by a lake
☐ by a river
☐ by a lake and by a river

c. Luzern's planetarium is
☐ very old
☐ very modern

d. Can you see the Alps from Luzern?
☐ yes
☐ no

e. How do you get to the top of the Pilatus mountain?
☐ by car
☐ by chair lift
☐ by cable car
☐ by chair lift or by cable car

3 Imagine you are a reporter who has recorded an interview with someone from Bielefeld – a town in north-west Germany. Listen through your interview a few times and jot down some notes under the key points below. (This is a fairly open-ended exercise; your notes do not have to correspond exactly to the answers on p. 174)

New vocabulary
die Lage location   **kleinstädtisch** provincial

a. Name der Stadt ....

b. Einwohner ....

c. Lage ....

e. Was ist los? ....

e. Atmosphäre ....

4 On the cassette you will hear an excerpt from a weather forecast, giving you information about three different areas in Germany. Listen carefully, then answer the questions below. (Answers p. 174)

a. Will there be snow in the mountains? ....

b. Will the temperatures in the Alps be below zero? ....

c. What will the weather be like in the Bavarian Forest? ....

....

d. Will it be very cloudy in North Germany? ....

Grammar

Making comparisons

You use **als** (than) when you compare two different things, e.g.

Memmingen ist kleiner als Ulm. Memmingen is smaller than Ulm.

Bier ist billiger als Wein. Beer is cheaper than wine.

In comparisons adjectives of one syllable with **a, o, u** usually modify these to *Umlauts*, i.e. **ä, ö, ü**, for example:

München ist groß. London ist größer als München.
Munich is big. London is bigger than Munich.

Irene ist elf Jahre alt. Mark ist vier Jahre älter als Irene.
Irene is eleven years old. Mark is four years older than Irene.

Herr Sommer ist sehr jung, aber seine Frau ist noch jünger.
Herr Sommer is very young, but his wife is even younger.

Exercise Make comparisons by the following the example. (Answers p. 174)

Example Compare the skirt with the trousers (skirt: 80 Marks, trousers 100 Marks)
Use **billig**

Der Rock ist billiger als die Hose

a. Compare Munich with Ulm
(Ulm: 100,000 inhabitants; Munich: 1.5 million inhabitants)
Use **groß**

....

b. Compare Maria with Hans
(Hans: 25 years old; Maria: 72 years old)
Use **alt**

....

c. Gerda with Claudia   Gerda: Claudia:
Use **dick** (fat)

....

d. The village with the city   village: city:
Use **ruhig**

....

Read and understand

1 This is a weather forecast from a newspaper. Study it, then tick the right boxes below. (Answers p. 174)

> **Vorhersage:** Am Samstag in Norddeutschland heiter bis wolkig und kaum Niederschläge; im Süden und in der Mitte wolkig bis start bewölkt und im Verlauf des Tages einsetzender Regen. Höchsttemperaturen 7 bis 12 Grad. Tiefstwerte in der Nacht zum Sonntag um 3 Grad; im Norden örtlich leichter Frost bis minus 3 Grad. Schwacher bis mäßiger Wind, vorwiegend aus östlichen Richtungen.

New vocabulary
Niederschläge (pl) rainfall
im Verlauf des Tages during the day
Tiefstwerte (pl) lowest temperatures
vorwiegend predominantly

a. Where is the weather going to be better on that particular day?

☐ in North Germany
☐ in South Germany

b. Is it going to rain a lot in North Germany?

☐ yes
☐ hardly at all

c. Where is it going to be colder at night?

☐ in North Germany
☐ in South Germany

2 Here is an advertisement about the holiday resort of Weggis in Switzerland. Study it, then tick the right boxes below. (Answers p. 174)

New vocabulary
Ferienwohnungen (pl) holiday apartments

> # WEGGIS
> **am Vierwaldstattersee**
> **der ruhige Urlaubsort**
> **mildes Klima**
> **ideal zum Baden, Wandern,**
> **Tennisspielen, Bootfahren**
> **27 Hotels – 1800 Betten – 200**
> **Ferienwohnungen**
>
> Auskunft und Prospekte
> Offiz. Verkehrsbüro CH-6353 Weggis
> Tel. 0041/41/93 1155 – Telex 78 395

a. What is the climate like?

☐ mild
☐ harsh

b. Is Weggis suitable for people wishing to spend a quiet holiday?

☐ yes
☐ no

c. Can you go swimming and boating there?

☐ yes
☐ no

Did you know?

Holiday areas in Austria and Switzerland

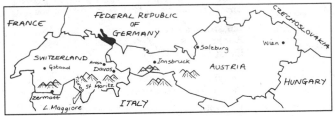

Austria (9 million inhabitants)

Austria (**Österreich**) is a well-established holiday country and has many
things to offer. First and foremost there are of course the Alps which cover
the west and the south of the country. Then there is the flat but charming
Burgenland south-east of Vienna which opens on to the vast Hungarian
plain. Vienna, Salzburg and Innsbruck are beautiful and interesting cities to
visit, and so are the numerous quiet little villages tucked away in the
mountains. Austria is popular with holidaymakers from all over Europe in
summer as well as in winter, so book well in advance if you plan to go
there. Austrians speak a dialect of German among themselves, which
foreigners (even Germans) find hard to understand, but at the same time
almost everybody can switch to 'proper German' when talking to people
from abroad.

Switzerland (6 million inhabitants)

Switzerland (**die Schweiz**) is another popular holiday country. German is
spoken by about 70 per cent of the population. If anything the Swiss
German dialect (**Schwyzerdütsch**) is even harder to understand than South
German and Austrian dialects, but again the Swiss will speak standard
German to foreigners. Some of the world's most famous (and most
expensive!) skiing resorts are in Switzerland, e.g. **St. Moritz, Zermatt,
Davos, Arosa, Gstaad**, etc. The Swiss Alps, running from the west to the
east of the country are rugged and spectacular, whereas mountains and
climate in the South in the Ticino region around Lake Maggiore are much
more gentle. In the Swiss Jura, north of the Alps, there are more mountains
of medium height.

For more information on these countries contact your travel agent, or the
national tourist offices (p. 239 for addresses)

Your turn to speak

1 Imagine you're from Brighton and someone is asking you about your town. Answer the questions. Michael will prompt you as usual. You'll practice:

Ich komme aus . . .
Brighton hat . . . Einwohner
Es ist ruhig/hektisch

2 This time you are at the tourist office asking about information about Vienna (**Wien**). You'll practice:

Was gibt es . . . zu sehen?
Gibt es. . .?

Revision/Review please turn to p. 220.

Answers

Practice what you have learned, p. 169 Exercise 1 You should have ticked (**a**), (**b**), (**e**), (**f**), (**g**), (**i**), (**k**), (**l**)

p. 170 Exercise 2(**a**) yes (**b**) by a lake and by a river (**c**) very modern (**d**) yes (**e**) by chair lift or by cable car.

p. 170 Exercise 3(**a**) Bielefeld (**b**) zirka 300 000 (**c**) am Teutoburger Wald (**d**) Es gibt Theater, Kinos, Kneipen (**e**) Kleinstädtisch
p. 170 Exercise 4(**a**) yes, locally (**b**) yes (**c**) cloudy, snow or snow showers (**d**) yes

Grammar Exercise p. 171 (**a**) München ist größer als Ulm (**b**) Maria ist älter als Hans (**c**) Gerda ist dicker als Claudia (**d**) Das Dorf ist ruhiger als die Stadt

Read and understand, p. 172 Exercise 1(**a**) in North Germany (**b**) hardly (**c**) in North Germany
p. 172 Exercise 2(**a**) mild (**b**) yes (**c**) yes.

13 More about yourself

What you will learn

- to talk about your hobbies, sports, special interests
- to describe where you live and where you lived before
- to describe the apartment or house you are living in
- to talk about your daily routine
- to talk about things which happened in the past

and you will be reading about three well-known German personalities.

2-Zimmer-Altbauwhg.
Parterre, sep. Eingang (reno-
vierungsbedürftig), in Blaubeuren zu vermieten.
Zuschriften unter Z 1439389

2-Zimmer-App.
(Wohnküche, Schlafzimmer)
komplett möbliert, Telefon, Ga-
rage, an soliden Herrn zu vermieten.
Zuschriften unter Z 1440064

2-Zimmer-Wohnung
Ulm-Söflingen zu vermieten.
Zuschriften unter Z 1438787

Study guide

	Dialogues 1, 2: listen straight through without the book
	Dialogues 1, 2: listen, read and study one by one
	Dialogues 3, 4: listen straight through without the book
	Dialogues 3, 4: listen, read and study one by one
	Dialogue 5: listen through without the book
	Dialogue 5: listen, read and study the notes
	Study the *Key words and phrases*
	Read the *Grammar* section and do the exercise
	Do the exercises in *Practice what you have learned*
	Do the exercises in *Read and understand*
	Read *Did you know?*
	Do the exercises in *Your turn to speak*
	Listen to all the dialogues once again straight through

Dialogues

 1 *Two little boys by the Danube on a rainy day. What are they doing?*

Ruth	Guten Tag!
Thomas	Guten Tag!
Robert	Tag!
Ruth	Was macht ihr denn?
Thomas	Oh, wir fischen.
Ruth	Fischen!!
Thomas und Robert	Ja.
Ruth	Habt ihr schon was gefangen?
Thomas und Robert	Nein, oh nein.
Thomas	Aber fast.
Ruth	Fast?
Thomas	Ja.
Ruth	Was denn?
Thomas und Robert	Oh – Stecken!
Ruth	Einen Stecken! Aha!

fischen to fish
der Stecken stick

 2 *Talking about hobbies*

Ruth	Und was machen Sie nach der Arbeit?
Frau Oswald	Ja, Hausarbeit, zum Teil auch mach ich meine Hobbys. Sport, zum Beispiel Schwimmen, Waldlauf. Dann interessiere ich mich vor allem für Sprachen. Ich interessiere mich für Reisen – der Ferne Osten, Südamerika.
Herr Schmid	Meine Hobbys sind Fotografieren, Briefmarkensammeln, dann einen kleinen Garten noch beim Haus – und wir halten uns durch sehr viel Wandern und durch Schwimmen fit.

- ◆ **die Hausarbeit** housework
- ◆ **das Hobby** hobby
- ◆ **der Sport** sport
- **der Waldlauf** jogging (cross-country)
- **vor allem** above all
- **der Ferne Osten** the far East
- ◆ **Fotografieren** photography
- ◆ **Briefmarkensammeln** collecting stamps
- **beim Haus** round the house.

1 **was macht ihr denn?** what are you doing? (Remember **machen** = to do, to make).

habt ihr schon was gefangen? have you caught anything yet?
fangen = to catch, **gefangen** = caught. See *Grammar* section for more details.

aber fast but almost.

was denn? what (then)?

2 **ich interessiere mich für ...** I'm interested in . . .

wir halten uns . . . fit we keep (ourselves) fit.

3 *Where does Herr Vollmert live?*

Ruth	Wo wohnen Sie?
Herr Vollmert	Ich wohne in Emmendingen.
Ruth	Wo ist das?
Herr Vollmert	In der Nähe von Freiburg.
Ruth	Wie lange wohnen Sie schon da?
Herr Vollmert	Hm, seit zwei Monaten etwa.
Ruth	Und wo haben Sie vorher gewohnt?
Herr Vollmert	Vorher habe ich drei Jahre lang in England gewohnt, in Bath.

4 *Rainer Schilz talks about his flat in Hamburg*

Herr Schilz Ich heiße Rainer Schilz, und ich bin Lehrer an einem Gymnasium in Hamburg. Ich wohne im Stadtzentrum, und zwar in einer großen Altbauwohnung. Die Wohnung hat vier Zimmer, Küche und Bad. Außerdem hab' ich noch einen Balkon, und von dort hat man einen sehr schönen Blick auf die Stadt und natürlich auch auf den Fluß. Vorher habe ich in einem Vorort gewohnt, und zwar in einer Neubauwohnung. Die Wohnung war kleiner, aber auch billiger. Die Wohnungen im Stadtzentrum sind für mich etwas teuer. Ich zahle zum Beispiel ungefähr 800 Mark im Monat. Trotzdem wohne ich viel lieber hier, und ich würde nicht gern wieder umziehen.

der Lehrer teacher
das Gymnasium grammar school
♦ **das Stadtzentrum** city centre
♦ **die Wohnung** apartment
♦ **die Küche** kitchen
außerdem besides
für mich for me

Interior of an 'Altbauwohnung' ♦

3 ♦ **und wo haben Sie vorher gewohnt?** and where did you live before that? (lit and where have you lived before that?)

♦ **vorher habe ich in Bath gewohnt** before that I lived in Bath.

4 ♦ **die Altbauwohnung** apartment in an old house. **Altbauwohnungen** are very much sought after, because they are usually larger and have more character

♦ than an apartment in a new house, **eine Neubauwohnung.** A great many Germans live in apartments rather than in houses, and most of these are rented. Only 38% of the population own the apartments or houses they live in.

von dort hat man einen sehr schönen Blick über die Stadt from there you have a fine view over the city.

♦ **vorher habe ich in einem Vorort gewohnt** before that I lived (lit. have lived) in a suburb.

trotzdem wohne ich viel lieber hier nevertheless I prefer to live here.

ich würde nicht gern wieder umziehen I wouldn't like to move again. (**umziehen** = to move)

☐ 5 *What's Herr Vollmert's day like?*

Ruth Was sind Sie von Beruf?

Herr Vollmert Ich bin Ingenieur, aber zur Zeit mache ich eine Pause, da meine Frau als Lehrerin arbeitet und ich auf unser Kind aufpasse.

Ruth Und wie sieht Ihr typischer Tag aus? Als Hausmann?

Herr Vollmert Hm – ich steh' am Morgen auf, zusammen mit meiner Frau, und zwar gegen etwa sieben Uhr, wenn uns das Kind weckt. Wir haben Frühstück zusammen, dann fährt meine Frau zur Schule; ich gehe mit dem Kind spazieren. Dann koch' ich zu Mittag für das Kind and für mich. Ja, dann am Nachmittag schläft das Kind meistens zwei Stunden, dann ruh ich mich auch etwas aus, lese etwas, lese die Zeitung. Nachmittags mache ich dann ab und zu schon mal wieder einen Spaziergang, und dann bringe ich das Kind zu Bett, und dann den Abend verbringe ich mit meiner Frau zusammen.

zur Zeit at the moment
der Ingenieur engineer
die Lehrerin female teacher
♦ **lesen** to read
♦ **die Zeitung** newspaper

ich mache eine Pause I'm taking a break.
da . . . ich auf unser Kind aufpasse since I'm looking after our child.
♦ **wie sieht Ihr typischer Tag aus?** what's a typical day like for you?

als Hausmann as a house-husband. This is a relatively new word; it has come into use to match **Hausfrau** (housewife).

♦ **ich stehe am Morgen auf** I get up in the morning. **Aufstehen** (to get up) is a separable verb

gegen etwa sieben Uhr round about seven o'clock.

wenn uns das Kind weckt when the child wakes us. **Wecken** = to wake, e.g. **ich wecke meine Frau um sieben** (I wake my wife at seven).

♦ **dann koche ich zu Mittag** then I cook lunch (lit. I cook for midday). Similarly: **dann koche ich zu Abend** then I cook supper (lit. I cook for the evening).

dann ruhe ich mich auch etwas aus then I have a rest as well.

♦ **nachmittags . . . mache ich . . . ab und zu . . . einen Spaziergang** in the afternoon I go for a walk every now and then. **Dann, schon, wieder** and **mal** are all 'filler' words without any special meaning.

dann bringe ich das Kind zu Bett then I put the child to bed.

♦ **den Abend verbringe ich mit meiner Frau zusammen** the evening I spend together with my wife.

Key words and phrases

Hobbies and pastimes

Meine Hobbys sind . . .	My hobbies are . . .
Sport	sports
Schwimmen	swimming
Waldlauf	jogging
Wandern	hiking
Fotografieren	photography
Briefmarkensammeln	collecting stamps
Ich interessiere mich für . . .	I'm interested in . . .
Sprachen	languages
Reisen	travelling

Where you live

Ich wohne . . .	I live . . .
im Stadtzentrum	in the city centre
in einem Vorort	in a suburb
in einer Altbauwohnung	in an old apartment
in einer Neubauwohnung	in a newly built apartment
Die Wohnung hat (vier) Zimmer, Küche und Bad	The apartment has (four) rooms, kitchen and bathroom.
Vorher habe ich in (Bath) gewohnt	Before I lived in (Bath)

A typical day

Ich stehe um sieben Uhr auf	I get up at seven o'clock
Dann . . .	Then . . .
mache ich meine Hausarbeit	I do my housework
lese ich Zeitung	I read the newspaper
koche ich zu Mittag	I cook lunch
Nachmittags mache ich einen Spaziergang	In the afternoon I go for a walk
Den Abend verbringe ich . . .	The evening I spend . . .
mit meiner Frau	with my wife
mit meinem Mann	with my husband
mit Freunden	with friends

Practice what you have learned

In these exercises you will hear people talk about the past, so it is a good idea to study the *Grammar* section *before* doing the listening exercises.

1 On tape you will hear Claudia talking about her lifestyle and her hobbies. Listen a few times, then tick the right boxes below. (Answers p. 188)

a. Claudia prefers to live

☐ in the city

☐ in the country

b. She prefers

☐ a quiet life

☐ a hectic life

c. She lives in

☐ a new apartment

☐ an old house

d. She likes to travel abroad

☐ yes

☐ no

e. Her hobbies are (tick four boxes)

☐ jazz

☐ photography

☐ reading

☐ walking

☐ films

☐ sport

2 On tape Herr Ott will be telling you about his daily routine. Listen a few times, then note what he does in the spaces provided. (Answers p. 188)

Time

a. 6:30 ....

b. 8:00 – 12:30 ....

c. 12:30 – 1:30 ....

d. 1:30 – 5:00 ....

e. After work ....

f. Often, around 8:00 ....

3 Herr Vollmert is telling Ruth about the time he spent in England. Listen to the dialogue a few times, then fill in the missing words in the spaces provided. You'll find the missing words jumbled up below. (Answers p. 188)

New vocabulary
unterrichten to teach   **angenehm** pleasant
die Landschaft countryside   **die Uni** (short for **die Universität**)

a. Ruth: Was haben Sie da gemacht?

b. Herr Vollmert: Ich habe dort an der ....

unterrichtet.

c. Und wie hat's Ihnen in .... gefallen?

d. Ah, in England hat's mir .... gefallen, und es

tut mir etwas leid, daß ich jetzt nicht mehr dort sein kann. Die

Landschaft hat mir gefallen, die Menschen fand ich sehr angenehm

– generell, das .... dort hat mir gut gefallen.

```
England          Uni

    sehr gut

        Leben
```

4 A woman is being interviewed about her last summer holidays. Listen to
the interview on tape, then write the answers to the questions below in the
boxes provided – in German. The letters in the numbered boxes will give
you the name of a country which is sometimes called 'Bavaria of the North'.
(Answers p. 188)

New vocabulary
die Abendschule evening class
Irland Ireland

a. Where did the woman go last summer?
b. What did she do there?
c. Does she speak Gaelic?
d. Where did she first learn English?
e. Where did she later learn English?
f. She learned most of her English by listening to . . . songs
g. How did Guinness taste to her?

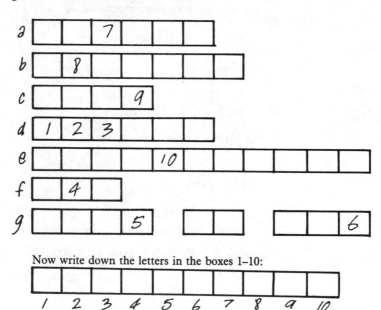

Now write down the letters in the boxes 1–10:

Grammar

The perfect tense

In English there are two ways of talking about the past. You can either say 'I have played' (grammar books call this the *perfect tense*) or 'I played' (*imperfect tense*). German has the same two patterns, but in German the perfect tense is more flexible than in English. For example in German you can say **Wo haben Sie vorher gewohnt?** (Where have you lived before? see dialogue 3), whereas in English you would have to say 'Where *did* you live before?' In everyday speech the perfect tense is widely used in Germany, so it is altogether more important than the imperfect.

Most verbs form the perfect with **haben** plus **ge-** before and **-t** after the verb stem. Let's take for example **wohnen** (to live).

haben +	ge [stem] t	
ich **habe**	ge wohn t	I have lived
du **hast**	ge wohn t	you have lived
er/sie/es **hat**	ge wohn t	he/she/it has lived
wir **haben**	ge wohn t	we have lived
ihr **habt**	ge wohn t	you have lived
sie/Sie **haben**	ge wohn t	they/you have lived

In English all verbs form their perfect tense with **haben**, but in German a few verbs use **sein** (to be). Dictionaries and verb lists usually state which verbs use **sein**. They often have to do with movement, e.g. **reisen** (to travel).

sein +	ge [stem] t	
ich **bin**	ge reis t	I have (lit. I am) travelled
du **bist**	ge reis t	you have (lit. you are) travelled
er/sie/es **ist**	ge reis t	he/she/it has (lit. is) travelled
wir **sind**	ge reis t	we have (lit. are) travelled
ihr **seid**	ge reis t	you have (lit. are) travelled
sie/Sie **sind**	ge reis t	they/you have (lit. are) travelled

Many verbs form their perfect tense in this way. But, as in English, there are a number of verbs in German which follow a different pattern. You have already come across **Habt ihr schon was gefangen?** (Have you caught anything yet?) in Dialogue 1. In this case **-en** instead of **-t** was added to the stem of the verb **fangen** (to catch). You will find more details about such verbs in Unit 14.

Exercise Write the perfect tense of the verbs **kaufen** (to buy) and **wandern** (to hike, to ramble) in the spaces below. The perfect tense of **kaufen** is formed with **haben** and that of **wandern** with **sein**. (The stem of **wandern** is **wander**, the stem of **kaufen** is **kauf**). (Answers p. 188)

kaufen	wandern
ich	ich ....
du	du ....
er/sie/es	er/sie/es ....
wir	wir ....
ihr	ihr ....
sie/Sie	sie/Sie ....

Read and understand

1 Match these lonely hearts' advertisements . . . who would suit whom?

New vocabulary
die Dame – lady
reif – mature
der Akademiker – professional gentleman
kultiviert – cultured

a.
> Dame von Welt, 39 Jahre, liebt Brahms und Goethe, sucht reifen Partner.

b.
> Tennis – Skifahren – Schwimmen – wo ist der dynamische Partner für dies und vieles mehr . . .?

c.
> Wo ist die Frau für mich, bin jung, aktiv, liebe Sport

d.
> Akademiker, Ende 50, sucht kultivierte Dame bis Ende 30

. . . . . goes with . . . . goes with . . . . .
(Answers p. 188)

2 Can you guess from this description whom we're talking about? **Wer ist es?**
(Answer p. 188)

New vocabulary
die Kindheit childhood
still quiet
schlecht bad

der akademische Posten academic post
das Patentamt patent office
die Entdeckung discovery
der Nobelpreis Nobel prize

> **Geboren in:** Ulm, 14.3.1879
> **Gestorben in:** Princeton, 18.4.1955
> **Kindheit:** Ulm: München; sehr stilles Kind (spricht erst mit 4 Jahren das erste Wort); sehr schlechter Schüler
> **Danach:** Italien; Schweiz; studiert in Bern, bekommt keinen akademischen Posten; arbeitet im Patentamt Bern.
> **1905** revolutionäre Entdeckung; über Nacht weltberühmt;
> **1921** Nobelpreis
> **1933** Emigration nach USA
> **Persönlichkeit:** viel Humor; liebt Musik; Pazifist

Did you know?

Martin Luther 1483–1546

Born in Eisleben, (now East Germany) the son of a miner. He became a monk in an Augustinian convent and was later ordained priest. His criticism of the Pope and his close and fresh reading of the Bible resulted in increasing controversies with the Established Catholic Church and led to his excommunication. His literary output was considerable and provided the basic creed for the Lutheran Church. (Today half of the population in Germany is Protestant, the other half Catholic). His sermons are still quoted, and his hymns still sung. His translation of the Bible into German is a powerful linguistic achievement and marks the emergence of German as a modern tongue.

Otto von Bismarck 1815–1898

German statesman and Prussian lord, known as the Iron Chancellor because of his authoritarian style of governing. After serving as an ambassador to St. Petersburg and Paris, he became Prussian prime minister and foreign minister, during which time he pushed the army reform through the Prussian Parliament. After wars against Austria and France, he founded the German Reich in 1871, at the exclusion of Austria and under the hegemony of Prussia, and became her first Imperial Chancellor. It was only through his forceful unification – economical and political – of the various small German states, that Germany was able to start playing a bigger role internationally. Abroad, Bismarck sought to secure a balance of power by means of an intricate system of alliances. At home, he became involved in conflicts with the Catholic Church and was a proclaimed enemy of socialism, the rise of which he tried to forestall by introducing social reform himself. In both these conflicts he was defeated. Friction with Kaiser Wilhelm II led to his dismissal in 1890.

Willy Brandt born 1913

German politician, educated at Lübeck and Oslo University. He emigrated in 1933 as an anti-Nazi and was active in the resistance. He resumed German citizenship in 1947, and in 1956 became mayor of West Berlin. A Social Democrat leader, he became foreign minister in 1966 and was Federal Chancellor from 1969–72. His period in office marked an important change in East-West relations. Brandt sought negotiations, talks and cultural exchanges with the East, which led to substantial improvements in East-West communications. He enjoys a very high international prestige and was awarded the Nobel Peace Prize in 1971. A more recent concern is his effort to ease tension in the world through his campaign to help the Third World countries, and to overcome the differences between North and South, as well as between the developed and the developing countries.

Your turn to speak

1   Someone is asking you where you live. Answer the questions according to
Michael's prompts.
You'll practice:

. . . einem Vorort
. . . in einer Neubauwohnung
. . . Zimmer, Küche, Bad
Es ist ruhig

2   Now you're talking about your daily routine and your hobbies.
You'll practice:

Ich stehe . . . auf
Morgens . . .
Nachmittags . . .
Abends . . .

Answers

Practice what you have learned p. 182 Exercise 1(a) in the city (b) a hectic
life (c) a new apartment (d) yes (e) jazz, photography, sport, reading

p. 183 Exercise 2(a) getting up, making breakfast, reading the paper
(b) work (c) eat lunch, go for a walk in the park (d) work, sometimes
there's a meeting (e) go shopping, cook supper (f) girl friend arrives, go
out to cinema, pub, theatre. dancing.

p. 183 Exercise 3(b) Uni (c) England (d) sehr gut, Leben.

p. 184 Exercise 4(a) Irland (b) wandern (c) nein (d) Schule (e)
Abendschule (f) Pop (g) Fast zu gut; the name of the country is
SCHOTTLAND (Scotland)

Grammar Exercise p. 185 **kaufen:** ich habe gekauft, du hast gekauft, er/sie/
es hat gekauft, wir haben gekauft, ihr habt gekauft, sie/Sie haben gekauft;
wandern: ich bin gewandert, du bist gewandert, er/sie/es ist gewandert, wir
sind gewandert, ihr seid gewandert, sie/Sie sind gewandert

Read and understand p. 186 Exercise 1(a) + (d) and (b) + (c)
Exercise 2 The person in question was **Albert Einstein**.

14 Talking about the past

What you will learn

- to understand what people have done in the recent past
- to talk about what happened to you in the past, e.g. on a holiday
- to understand an anecdote set in 19th century Ulm about an early attempt to fly

and you will read something about the history of Germany.

Flugmaschine

Verfertiget von Berblinger in Ulm

Ansicht des Profils.

Study guide

	Dialogue 1: listen straight through without the book
	Dialogue 1: listen, read and study notes
	Dialogues 2, 3: listen straight through without the book
	Dialogues 2, 3: listen, read and study one by one
	Dialogue 4: listen straight through without the book
	Dialogue 4: listen, read and study notes
	Study the *Key words and phrases*
	Read the *Grammar* section
	Do the exercises in *Practice what you have learned*
	Do the exercise in *Read and understand*
	Read *Did you know?*
	Do the exercises in *Your turn to speak*
	Listen to all the dialogues once again straight through

1 *Agnes tells Ruth about her trip to India*

Ruth   Agnes, wo bist du im letzten Urlaub gewesen?

Agnes   Ich bin nach Indien gefahren.

Ruth   Und bist du alleine gereist?

Agnes   Zum Teil. Meine Freundin fuhr schon eine Woche vorher weg, und wir haben uns in Delhi getroffen, und sind von da aus gemeinsam weitergereist. Und nach etwa vier Wochen haben sich unsere Wege wieder getrennt, und ich bin nach Sri Lanka und sie ist nach Nepal gefahren.

Ruth   Bist du dann alleine gereist?

Agnes   Dann bin ich alleine gereist. Ja.

Ruth   Wie hat das geklappt?

Agnes   Das hat ganz gut geklappt. Eh – natürlich ist es angenehmer wenn man zu zweit reist, aber im großen und ganzen hat das ganz gut geklappt.

Ruth   Ja – vielleicht war's auch ein bißchen schwieriger, als Frau alleine zu reisen?

Agnes   Ich glaube nicht. Ich fand es leichter, in Indien allein als Frau zu reisen als in manchen südeuropäischen Ländern.

allein(e) alone
gemeinsam together

Große Studienreise durch Nordindien und Nepal
Geheimnisvolles Land zwischen Tibet und Indien.

Südindien – Sri Lanka
Entlang der südindischen Tempel-straße und durch das Tropenparadies Ceylon.

Auf der Tempelstraße durch Südindien und mit der Fähre nach Sri Lanka (Ceylon).

20 Tage Studien- und Erlebnisreise

Südindien: Madras – Kanchipuram – Mahabali-puram – Pondicherry – Auroville – Chidambaram –

1 ◆ **wo bist du im letzten Urlaub gewesen?** where did you go (lit. where have you been) for your last holiday? **Gewesen** = been, from **sein** (= to be), see *Grammar* section.

◆ **ich bin nach Indien gefahren** I went to India. In German you can use the perfect tense and say 'I have gone to India' (lit. I am gone, because **fahren** (to go, to travel) uses **sein** to form its perfect.)

meine Freundin fuhr . . . my girl friend went . . . **fuhr** is the imperfect tense of **fahren** (see *Grammar* section).

◆ **wir haben uns in Delhi getroffen** we met (lit. have met) in Delhi (**getroffen** from **treffen** = to meet).

wir sind . . . weitergereist we travelled . . . on.

unsere Wege . . . haben sich wieder getrennt our paths separated again. **Trennen** = to separate, to divide, **der Weg** = path, way.

◆ **wie hat das geklappt?** how did that work out? (**klappen** = to work out).

◆ **das hat ganz gut geklappt** that went quite well.

zu zweit with someone else (from **zwei** = two).

im großen und ganzen on the whole.

als Frau as a woman. Similarly: **als Mann** (as a man).

ich glaube nicht I don't think so. **Glauben** = to believe, to think.

ich fand es leichter I found it easier.

in manchen südeuropäischen Ländern in some southern European countries.

2 *Ruth asks Herr Schuster about his trip to Berlin*

Ruth | Was haben Sie an Ostern gemacht?
Herr Schuster | Ostern bin ich mit einer Gruppe englischer Studenten nach Berlin gefahren.
Ruth | Und warum? Was haben Sie da gemacht?
Herr Schuster | Ah, wir haben deutsche Firmen besichtigt.
Ruth | Und wie hat's den Studenten gefallen?
Herr Schuster | Oh, die Studenten waren begeistert, es war sehr schön in Berlin.

warum why
begeistert enthusiastic, thrilled

3 *What did the students do in the evening in Berlin?*

Ruth | Wie war das Wetter?
Herr Schuster | Ah, das Wetter war wunderbar. Die Leute waren sehr freundlich – rundum, es war ein schöner Besuch.
Ruth | Mhm. Und was haben Sie sonst noch alles gemacht? Abends zum Beispiel?
Herr Schuster | Ja, abends sind wir an den Kudamm gegangen, das ist eine der schönsten Straßen in Berlin. Wir haben gegessen dort, wir sind in Diskotheken gegangen, wir sind ins Kino gegangen, ins Theater gegangen, die Studenten haben natürlich auch in Tanzlokalen getanzt, und ab und zu haben sie auch schon mal zu viel getrunken, und sind dann – ich glaube einmal – zu spät ins Hotel gekommen.

rundum all round
der Besuch visit, stay
zu viel too much
zu spät too late

*Street cafes along the
Kurfürstendamm in Berlin*

2

an Ostern at Easter. You will hear **an Ostern** in southern Germany. In north
♦ Germany people say **zu Ostern**. You can also just say
♦ **was haben Sie Ostern gemacht?** Similarly:
(zu) Weihnachten (at Christmas).

wir haben deutsche Firmen besichtigt we visited German firms. **Die Firma**
= firm; **besichtigen** = to visit in order to have a look at something, e.g.
♦ **wir haben das Rathaus besichtigt** we had a look at the town hall.

wie hat's den Studenten gefallen? how did the students like it?
Remember **wie gefällt es dir/Ihnen?** from Unit 12. **Hat . . . gefallen** is the
perfect tense of **gefallen** (to please, to like). *You* would be asked:
♦ **wie hat es Ihnen gefallen?** and you would answer
♦ **es hat mir/uns gut gefallen** (I/we liked it a lot).

3

wie was das Wetter? what was the weather like?

was haben Sie sonst noch alles gemacht? what else did you do?

der Kudamm short for **der Kurfürstendamm**. The **Kurfürstendamm** is
West Berlin's most famous boulevard with many fashionable shops and
restaurants.

♦ wir sind . . . gegangen we went.
♦ wir haben . . . gegessen we ate.
♦ sie haben . . . getanzt they danced.
♦ sie haben . . . getrunken they drank.

sind dann . . . zu spät ins Hotel gekommen were late coming back to the
hotel.

4 Der Schneider von Ulm (The Tailor of Ulm)

Agnes Der Schneider von Ulm, das war eine bekannte historische Persönlichkeit. Er kam aus einer armen Familie, war sehr genial, und hat in Ulm gelebt; und Anfang des 19. Jahrhunderts hat er probiert zu fliegen, der alte Menschheitstraum. Er hat an der schwäbischen Alb verschiedene Probeflüge gemacht und hatte zum Teil auch Erfolg damit, und als dann 1810 der König von Württemberg Ulm besuchte, sollte natürlich der Schneider zeigen, daß er fliegen konnte. Man baute Tribünen auf, hoch über die Donau, der Schneider stieg hinauf, aber leider klappte das mit dem Fliegen nicht. Er flog nicht sehr weit und nach wenigen Metern stürzte er bereits ins Wasser, und natürlich sein ganzes Prestige war dahin, er wurde vielmehr zur Spottfigur der ganzen Stadt und kam damit zu einem tragischen Ende. Erst viel viel später sah man, wie genial seine Erfindung doch eigentlich war.

genial ingenious	**die Tribüne** platform
der Menschheitstraum dream of mankind	**wenig** a few
	bereits already
der König the king	

eine bekannte historische Persönlichkeit a well-known figure in history.

er kam aus einer armen Familie he came from a poor family. When giving a factual account of what happened way back in the past, the *imperfect* rather than the *perfect* is used. We have included this short narrative episode to demonstrate this. The most important tense for *you* to talk about the past though is the perfect, because it is more colloquial and deals with recent events.

Anfang des 19. Jahrhunderts at the beginning of the 19th century.

er hat probiert zu fliegen he has tried to fly.

verschiedene Probeflüge several test flights.

. . . hatte . . . Erfolg damit . . . had success with it.

. . . sollte der Schneider zeigen the tailor should show.

daß er fliegen konnte that he could fly. Note that after **daß** the modal verb **konnte** (could; from **können** = can) goes to the *end* of the sentence.

der Schneider stieg hinauf the tailor climbed up.

er flog he flew.

er stürzte he crashed, he fell.

sein ganzes Prestige war dahin his whole prestige was gone.

er wurde vielmehr zur Spottfigur der ganzen Stadt he became a figure of fun all over town.

zu einem tragischen Ende to a tragic end.

erst viel viel später sah man only much, much later one saw.

wie genial seine Erfindung doch eigentlich war how ingenious his invention in fact was. **Die Erfindung** = invention, **erfinden** = to invent.

Key words and phrases

To understand

Wo bist du/sind Sie im letzten Urlaub gewesen?	Where did you go for your last holiday?
Was haben Sie Ostern/ Weihnachten gemacht?	What did you do for Easter/ Christmas?
Wie hat das geklappt?	How did that work out?
Wie hat es Ihnen gefallen?	How did you like it?
Wie war das Wetter?	What was the weather like?

To use

Ich bin nach Indien/Berlin gefahren	I went to India/Berlin
Wir haben uns in Delhi getroffen	We met up in Delhi
Wir haben die Stadt besichtigt	We had a look at the town
Wir haben dort . . .	There we . . .
gegessen	ate
getrunken	drank
getanzt	danced
Wir sind in Diskotheken/ins Theater gegangen	We went to discotheques/to the theatre
Das hat (ganz) gut geklappt	It worked out (quite) well
Es hat uns gut gefallen	We liked it a lot
Wir waren begeistert	We were thrilled
Das Wetter war schön/wunderbar	The weather was fine/wonderful

Practice what you have learned

Read the *Grammar* section before doing the exercises

1 A young man is talking about his latest Christmas holiday. You can read what he says below. Fill in the missing words (from the box) first, then listen to the tape to check whether you were right.

Weihnachten bin ich in Spanien .... Ich

bin mit einer Spanierin .... und ihre

Familie .... in der Nähe von Barcelona.

Wir sind oft nach Barcelona .... und

haben die Stadt .... Abends waren wir

dann mit der Familie zusammen; wir haben zu Abend

.... und haben dazu Wein

.... Das Wetter war schön, und es hat

uns gut ....

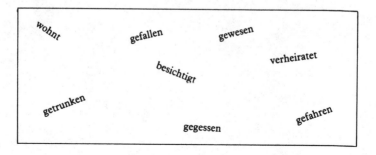

wohnt   gefallen   gewesen

besichtigt   verheiratet

getrunken

gegessen   gefahren

2 On tape you'll hear two people talking about their latest holidays. Listen several times, then answer the questions below. (Answers p. 202)

a. What did Irma do? ....

b. Was her holiday quiet or hectic? ....

c. Did she like it? ....

d. Where did Heinz go for his holiday? ....

e. Why didn't he like it? ....

3 Agnes tells Ruth a few more things about her trip to India. Listen to their conversation, then tick the right boxes below. (Answers p. 202)

New vocabulary
man muß aufpassen one must be careful
rohe Früchte fresh fruit

a. Wie ist Agnes gefahren?

☐ mit dem Bus und mit dem Zug

☐ nur mit dem Bus

b. Wie hat Agnes das Essen geschmeckt?

☐ gut

☐ nicht sehr gut

c. Darf man rohe Früchte essen?

☐ ja

☐ nein

d. Wer war krank?

☐ Agnes

☐ die Freundin von Agnes

4 A young man is being asked what he did last week. Listen to his replies, then match up the pictures below the diary with the appropriate day of the week, e.g. fill in **a**, **b**, **c**, etc. (Answers p. 202)

Grammar

The imperfect tense

Sentences like **ich wohnte in Ulm** (I lived in Ulm) or **ich reiste nach Indien** (I travelled to India) use the imperfect tense to describe something that happened in the past. There are no fixed rules, but in everyday speech you would probably use the perfect tense and say **ich habe in Ulm gewohnt** (lit. I have lived in Ulm) and **ich bin nach Indien gereist** (I have travelled to India), but, although less common, it is useful to recognize the imperfect. The imperfect of most verbs is easy to form. You just insert **-t** after the stem, e.g. **wohnen** (to live):

ich **wohnte**	I lived	wir **wohnten**	we lived
du **wohntest**	you lived	ihr **wohntet**	you lived
er/sie/es **wohnte**	he, she, it lived	Sie/sie **wohnten**	you/they lived

Strong verbs

These verbs form their imperfect in a different way. Instead of inserting **-t** after the stem (see above) they change their stem altogether – just as several English verbs do. Sometimes the English and German verbs are closely related and change in a similar way, e.g.

to sing	**singen**	sang	**sang**	sung	**gesungen**
to drink	**trinken**	drank	**trank**	drunk	**getrunken**

But more often than not there is little resemblance between these 'strong' verbs in German and English. You'll have to recognize and learn them as you come across them. We can't list them all here – there are over 100! – but you'll find a complete list in dictionaries. And here are a few examples of strong verbs in the imperfect and perfect as they occurred in this unit:

Imperfect

fahren (to travel, to go somewhere)
Meine Freundin fuhr eine Woche vorher.
My friend went a week earlier.

kommen (to come)
Er kam aus einer armen Familie.
He came from a poor family

Perfect

gehen (to go, to walk)
Wir sind ins Theater gegangen.
We went (lit. have gone) to the theatre.

essen (to eat)
Die Studenten haben in Restaurants gegessen.
The students ate (lit. have eaten) in restaurants.

sein and *haben*

With these two important verbs the imperfect is more widely used than the perfect, but here is a list of both imperfect and perfect forms:

	sein		**haben**	
	imperfect	*perfect*	*imperfect*	*perfect*
ich	war	bin gewesen	hatte	habe gehabt
du	warst	bist gewesen	hattest	hast gehabt
er, sie, es	war	ist gewesen	hatte	hat gehabt
wir	waren	sind gewesen	hatten	haben gehabt
ihr	wart	seid gewesen	hattet	habt gehabt
Sie/sie	waren	sind gewesen	hatten	haben gehabt

Read and understand

The Wagners from Hamburg are on holiday in Swabia (**Schwaben**). Read this letter Mrs. Wagner has written to her daughter, then write (in English) what they did yesterday, today and last Saturday in the spaces provided. (Answers p. 202)

New vocabulary
nett nice **Mutti** Mommy **Vati** Daddy

Ulm, den 12. August

Liebe Anke,

viele Grüße aus Schwaben. Wir sind hier im Hotel 'Pichler'.
Heute morgen haben wir einen Ausflug nach Blaubeuren gemacht und
dort das Kloster besichtigt. Gestern waren wir den ganzen Tag im
Schwarzwald und sind viel gewandert. Es war wunderschönes Wetter.
Gestern abend war ich sehr müde und bin schon um neun Uhr ins
Bett gegangen. Letzten Samstag haben wir Maria und ihren Mann
in Tübingen besucht. Sie haben uns die Stadt gezeigt, und wir
haben eine Bootsfahrt auf dem Fluß gemacht. Abends gab es dann
eine Party, und wir haben viele nette Leute getroffen. Am
Wochenende sind wir wieder zu Hause.

Deine

Mutti
Grüße auch von Vati!

Today

....

....

....

Yesterday

....

....

....

Last Saturday

....

....

....

Did you know?

Some German history

Germany has nearly always had a strong regional tradition. It used to consist of many different, often tiny, states which at some times were more united than at others. The first German Empire (**Reich**) flourished in the Middle Ages under the successors of Charlemagne and the **Hohenstaufen** emperors. It covered a huge area, comprising Germany, Austria, parts of France and Italy and what are now parts of Poland, Czechoslovakia and Hungary. The Emperors of this **Reich** saw themselves as successors to the Roman empire and called their realm the 'Holy Roman Empire'. Officially the Holy Roman Empire lasted until 1806 when Napoleon dissolved it. But it had begun to decline a long time before, especially after the Thirty Years' War (1618–1648).

Prussia and the Second German Empire of 1871

After the Thirty Years' War, Prussia and Austria emerged as the two most powerful states within the Holy Roman Empire. The Prussian king Frederick II and the Austrian empress Maria Theresa fought long wars against each other in the 18th century, and after the Napoleonic wars the old rivalry continued in the 19th century. It was Prussia under Bismarck who fought a final war against the Austrians and defeated them in 1866. Bismarck then founded a German Empire without Austria in 1871. The Prussian king Wilhelm became its emperor (**Kaiser**), and Bismarck became chancellor. Austria meanwhile remained a powerful empire on its own. The dual monarchy of Austria and Hungary was founded in 1867, and Austria actually became Germany's ally in the First World War (1914–1918).

Germany between the wars

After the First World War the **Kaiser** (Wilhelm II) abdicated, and Germany became a republic – called the **Weimar** Republic. But in 1933 the National Socialists under Hitler came into power, and the period of the infamous **Third Reich** began. Hitler annexed Austria (a republic since 1918) in 1938, and invaded Poland in 1939. This led to the Second World War.

Postwar Germany

After her surrender in 1945 Germany was divided into four 'zones', occupied by Britain, the United States, France and the Soviet Union. In 1949 the three western zones were merged and the Federal Republic was founded. Konrad Adenauer was the first chancellor. In the Soviet zone the German Democratic Republic was founded and established its capital in East Berlin. (The British, American and French sectors of Berlin, however, although geographically in East Germany, remained closely affiliated to the Federal Republic). In the fifties and sixties there was a great deal of tension between the two Germanys which culminated in the building of the Berlin Wall in 1961 by the East German government. Willy Brandt tried to improve relations with his **Ostpolitik**, and in 1973 a basic treaty between East and West Germany was signed. In the same year both countries were admitted as two independent states to the United Nations. Changes within the Soviet block states resulted in the opening of the Berlin Wall in November, 1989 and the reunification of the two states in October, 1990.

Your turn to speak

1 Someone is asking you about your last holiday. Answer according to Michael's prompts. You'll practice:

Wir sind nach . . . gefahren
Wir waren . . .
Gegessen, getrunken, getanzt

2 This time you'll answer some questions about your weekend. You'll practice:

Es war nicht . . .
Ich habe . . . besucht, gearbeitet
Es hat geregnet (it rained)
Ich bin . . . gegangen, gefahren

Answers

Practice what you have learned p. 197 Exercise 2(a) she stayed at home (b) quiet (c) yes (d) Brasil (e) it was too hot and the food wasn't nice

p. 197 Exercise 3(a) mit dem Bus und mit dem Zug (b) nicht sehr gut (c) nein (d) die Freundin von Agnes

p. 198 Exercise 4 Montag(f) Dienstag(b) Mittwoch(e) Donnerstag(g) Freitag(d) Samstag(c) Sonntag(a)

Read and understand p. 200 **Today:** Trip to Blaubeuren to see the monastery **Yesterday:** Walking in the Black forest, gone to bed at nine **Last Saturday:** Gone to see Maria and her husband, boat trip on the river, party in the evening, met nice people.

15 Stating your intentions

What you will learn

- to ask people about their future plans
- how to invite someone out for an evening
- to talk about your own plans
  and you will read something about how the Germans spend their free time.

Study guide

	Dialogues 1–3: listen straight through without the book
	Dialogues 1–3: listen, read and study one by one
	Dialogues 4, 5: listen through without the book
	Dialogues 4, 5: listen, read and study one by one
	Dialogue 6: listen through without the book
	Dialogue 6: listen, read and study the notes
	Study the *Key words and phrases*
	Do the exercises in *Practice what you have learned*
	Read the *Grammar* section
	Do the exercise in *Read and understand*
	Read *Did you know?*
	Do the exercises in *Your turn to speak*
	Listen to all the dialogues once again straight through

1 *Ursula talks to Ingrid Paplawski about her day*

Ursula Ingrid, was machst du heute? Hast du frei, oder mußt du arbeiten?

Ingrid Nein, heute hab' ich frei, Gott sei Dank. Heute morgen gehe ich erst mal einkaufen, und dann zum Friseur . . . Ja, und dann ist schon Mittag. Ich werde etwas zu Hause essen, und dann abwaschen und die Wohnung ein bißchen aufräumen. Heute nachmittag gehe ich mit dem Hund spazieren, und dann so um vier werden ein paar Freundinnen zum Kaffee kommen. Um halb sechs kommt dann schon mein Mann von der Arbeit nach Hause. Heute abend machen wir nichts – wir sehen uns wahrscheinlich einen guten Film im Fernsehen an.

Gott sei Dank thank God
♦ **der Friseur** hairdresser

2 *An invitation to a concert*

Hermann Ich geh' heute abend ins Konzert. Hast du Lust mitzugehen?
Cordula Ja gerne. Was gibt es denn?
Hermann Klavierkonzerte, Tschaikowsky –
Cordula Und wo?
Hermann Das ist in der Stadthalle.
Cordula Um wieviel Uhr denn?
Hermann Um acht Uhr.
Cordula O ja, gut. Wann treffen wir uns denn dann?
Hermann Um halb acht im 'Bürgereck'.
Cordula Gut. Kaufst du die Karten?
Hermann Ja. Welcher Preis? Sie kosten zwischen 15 und 20.
Cordula Och, nimm so mittlere Preislage.
Hermann Okay.
Cordula Gut. Bis dann.
Hermann Tschüß!
Cordula Tschüß!

das Klavierkonzert piano concerto
die Stadthalle municipal hall

1

- **hast du frei?** have you got the day off? (lit. have you free).

- **heute habe ich frei** today I'm off.

- **. . . gehe ich erst mal einkaufen . . .** first I go shopping. **Erst** (short for **zuerst**) = first; **mal** is a 'filler'.

- **ich werde etwas zu Hause essen** I'll eat something at home. Here is an example of the future tense, formed with **werden** + verb: **ich werde essen** (I'll eat). But you do not necessarily have to use this tense when you want to state your future intentions. More often than not, especially for events in the *near* future, you use the present tense in German, e.g. Ingrid says in the next sentence: **heute nachmittag gehe ich mit dem Hund spazieren** (this afternoon I take the dog for a walk). See *Grammar* section for more details about the future.

- **abwaschen** to wash up. **Abwaschen** is a separable verb: **ich wasche ab** (I wash up). But after **werden** it joins up again: **ich werde abwaschen** (I'll wash up).

- **aufräumen** to tidy ab. Another separable verb: **ich räume die Wohnung auf** (I tidy up the flat), but: **ich werde die Wohnung aufräumen** (I'll tidy up the flat).

  . . . kommt . . . mein Mann von der Arbeit nach Hause . . . my husband comes back home from work. Again the present tense is used for a future event.

- **heute abend machen wir nichts** tonight we're not doing anything (lit. we do nothing).

  wir sehen uns . . . einen guten Film . . . an we'll watch a good film (lit. we watch a good film). **Ansehen** (to watch) is a separable verb.

2

- **hast du Lust, mitzugehen?** do you feel like coming (lit. going) along? Similarly:
  hast du Lust, ins Kino zu gehen? do you feel like going to the cinema?
  haben Sie Lust, zum Essen zu kommen? do you feel like coming for supper? If you don't feel like it, you say
- **ich habe keine Lust.**

  wann treffen wir uns? when shall we meet? (lit. when meet we us?)

  Bürgereck name of a pub.

  nimm so mittlere Preislage take a medium price range. **Nimm** = from **nehmen** (to take).

  bis dann till then, see you then. Similarly: **bis morgen** (see you tomorrow).

  tschüß informal way of saying good-bye.

3 *What's Herr Schilz going to do on the weekend?*

Ursula Herr Schilz, was machen Sie am Wochenende?

Herr Schilz Ich habe diese Woche viel gearbeitet, und ich möchte gern ein ruhiges Wochenende. Ich wohne mit meiner Freundin zusammen, und wir werden viel Zeit zu Hause verbringen. Wir kochen, spielen Karten, lesen, faulenzen. . . . Samstagabend gehen wir wahrscheinlich ins 'Quartier Latin'. Das ist meine Stammkneipe, und da treffen wir immer unsere Freunde. Am Sonntag wird es dann wohl etwas hektischer. Da kommen ein paar Freunde zu Besuch; die bringen auch ihre Kinder mit, und dann wird es wohl schon etwas lauter werden.

- **faulenzen** to laze about, to relax
  die Stammkneipe local (pub)
- **zu Besuch** to visit

4 *Ursula talks to Irene and Ingrid about their holiday plans*

Ursula Ingrid, hast du schon Urlaubspläne für diesen Sommer?

Ingrid Ich mache nie im Sommer Urlaub, da ist es mir zu voll. Ich fahre im Frühjahr oder im Herbst weg, und manchmal fahre ich noch im Winter zum Skilaufen.

Ursula Und du, Irene? Was machst du im Urlaub?

Irene Ich werde im Juni nach Portugal fahren. Ein Freund von mir hat dort ein Haus – direkt am Strand. Ich möchte nur in der Sonne liegen, schwimmen und faulenzen.

Ursula Und fliegst du dahin, oder fährst du mit der Bahn oder mit dem Auto?

Irene Ich werde mit dem Flugzeug nach Lissabon fliegen und mir dort ein Auto mieten.

- **Urlaubspläne** (pl) holiday plans
  zu voll too crowded
  Skilaufen = Skifahren
- **am Strand** by the beach
  (**der Strand** = beach)

3 ♦ **wir spielen Karten** we'll play cards. Similarly: **wir spielen Golf** (we'll play golf), **wir spielen Tennis** (we'll play tennis). Several verbs in this dialogue are in the present with future meaning.

Quartier Latin name of a pub.

am Sonntag wird es dann wohl etwas hektischer it will be a bit more hectic on Sunday. **Wird** is a form of **werden**.

die bringen auch ihre Kinder mit they'll bring their children along. **Mitbringen** (to bring along) is a separable verb.

dann wird es . . . etwas lauter werden then it will become a bit more noisy. He could have omitted the second **werden** and simply have said **dann wird es etwas lauter.** (See above: **dann wird es etwas hektischer**). See *Grammar* section for more details on **werden.**

4 **mit der Bahn** by train. You know **der Zug; die Bahn** is another word for train. (See **Deutsche Bundesbahn** – German Federal Railway).

♦ **ich werde . . . (mir) dort ein Auto mieten** I'll rent (myself) a car there.

5   *And what is Rainer Schilz going to do for his holiday?*

Ursula   Und Herr Schilz, was für Urlaubspläne haben Sie?
Herr Schilz   Ja, wir werden dieses Jahr unsere große Reise machen, und zwar
fahren wir für sechs Wochen nach Südamerika.
Ursula   Das ist ja toll! Und wohin fahren Sie da?
Herr Schilz   Wir werden nach Rio fliegen und eine Weile dort bleiben. Von da
fahren wir dann mit dem Bus über Land. Das ist am billigsten
und man sieht auch am meisten, und man lernt Land und Leute
kennen.

Südamerika South America
toll fantastic
Rio = Rio de Janeiro

6   *Agnes' future plans*

Ruth   Agnes, was für Pläne hast du für die Zukunft?
Agnes   Ich habe einen Vertrag bis nächstes Jahr im Juli, hier in dieser
Stadt, und werde bis dahin arbeiten.
Ruth   Und danach?
Agnes   Eh, das ist noch ungewiß. Vielleicht werde ich freiberuflich
arbeiten, oder vielleicht werde ich auch etwas ganz anderes
machen. Vielleicht werden wir an Kinder denken – nicht wahr?
Barry   Ja.

♦ **die Zukunft** the future
der Vertrag contract
danach after that
freiberuflich freelance

5   **unsere große Reise** our big trip.

wir werden . . . eine Weile dort bleiben we'll stay there for a while.

♦ **über Land** overland.

♦ **man lernt Land und Leute kennen** one gets to know (lit. one learns to know) the country and the people.

6 ♦ **was für Pläne hast du. . .?** what plans have you got? (**der Plan** = plan)

bis dahin until then.

noch ungewiß still uncertain. As in English, **un-** often denotes the opposite, e.g. **gewiß – ungewiß** (certain – uncertain), **glücklich – unglücklich** (happy – unhappy), **klar – unklar** (clear – unclear).

♦ **etwas ganz anderes** something completely different.

Key words and phrases

Hast du/haben Sie heute frei?	Are you off today?
(Ja), heute habe ich frei	(Yes), I'm off today
Ich werde . . .	I'll . . .
einkaufen gehen	go shopping
zum Friseur gehen	go to the hairdresser
abwaschen	wash up
aufräumen	tidy up
spazieren gehen	go for a walk
Heute abend machen wir nichts	Tonight we won't do anything
Hast du/haben Sie Lust. . .	Do you feel like. . .
ins Kino zu gehen?	going to the cinema?
mitzugehen?	coming along?
zum Essen zu kommen?	coming for dinner?
Ja, gerne.	Yes, with pleasure.
Nein, ich habe keine Lust.	No, I don't feel like it.
Wir faulenzen	We'll laze about
Wir spielen Karten	We'll play cards
Ein paar Freunde kommen zu Besuch	A few friends will come to visit
Was für Urlaubspläne haben Sie?	What kind of holiday plans have you got?
Wir werden nach . . . fahren/ fliegen	We'll go/fly to . . .
Ich werde . . .	I'll . . .
über Land fahren	travel overland
mir ein Auto mieten	rent a car
nur am Strand liegen	just lie on the beach
Was für Pläne hast du/haben Sie für die Zukunft?	What plans have you got for the future?
Vielleicht werde ich etwas ganz anderes machen	Perhaps I'll do something completely different

Practice what you have learned

1 Ruth asks Jan about his plans for the weekend. Listen to their conversation on tape, then decide whether the statements below are true or false. (**Richtig oder Falsch**). (Answers p. 216)

New vocabulary
da freue ich mich drauf I'm looking forward to it
das Turnier tournament

a. There's a soccer game, but he's not looking forward to it. ⬚ **R** ⬚ **F**

b. There's a soccer game and he's looking forward to it, although he isn't a good player. ⬚ **R** ⬚ **F**

c. He's not a good player because he smokes and drinks too much. ⬚ **R** ⬚ **F**

2 It's Friday morning, and Wanda is telling you about her plans for the day and the next two days. Listen to her, then fill in her diary for her – in German. (Answers p. 216)

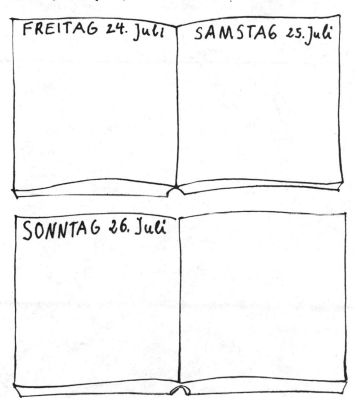

FREITAG 24. Juli   SAMSTAG 25. Juli

SONNTAG 26. Juli

3 On tape you will hear five people being asked about their future plans. Listen carefully, then write down below (in German) when they'll be doing what. (Answers p. 216)

	Who?	When?	What?
a.	Anna	nächstes Jahr	in Bonn studieren
b.	Richard		
c.	Frl. Braun		
d.	Herr Lange		
e.	Frau Columbus		

4 Herr Schmidt asks Frl. Johann to go to the theatre with him. Listen to their conversation, then answer the questions below. (Answers p. 216)

a. Has Herr Schmidt already bought the tickets? ....

b. Has Frl. Johann got time to come along? ....

c. What's the title of the play? ....

d. Is it a modern play or a classic? ....

e. What would Frl. Johann rather do? ....

f. Is she quite willing to go out with Herr Schmidt another time?

....

Grammar

The future

The future tense is formed with **werden** (which here has the meaning of 'shall', 'will' or 'going to') plus the verb, e.g.

Ich werde etwas essen. I'll eat something.
Wir werden viel Zeit zu Hause verbringen. We'll spend a lot of time at home.
Ich werde im Sommer nach Portugal fahren. I'll go to Portugal in the summer.

Note that after **werden** the second verb goes to the *end* of the sentence.

Here are all the forms of **werden:**

ich werde	I shall/will
du wirst	you will
er, sie, es wird	he, she, it will
wir werden	we shall/will
ihr werdet	you will
Sie/sie werden	You/they will

Werden on its own often has the meaning of 'to get, to become', e.g.

Ich werde krank.	I'm getting ill.
Wir werden naß.	We're getting wet.

Very often the present is used to state future intentions, e.g.

Wir treffen uns heute abend.	We'll meet tonight.
Am Sonntag kommen ein paar Freunde.	A few friends will come on Sunday.
Wir fliegen im Sommer nach Rio.	We'll fly to Rio in the summer.

Or you could use **möchte** or **wollen** to state a (slightly stronger) future intention:

Heute abend möchte ich ausgehen.	I'd like to go out tonight.
Ich will morgen zu Hause bleiben.	I want to stay at home tomorrow.

Note that **ich will** means 'I want to' and not just 'I will'.

Read and understand

Ursula, an Aries (**Widder**), and Michael, a Scorpio (**Skorpion**) are reading their horoscopes. Can you understand them as well and tick the right boxes below? (Answers p. 216)

Widder 21. März – 20. April

Skorpion 24. Oktober – 22. November

> Ihre schwierige Zeit ist vorbei. Nun wird es leichter für Sie – vor allem im Beruf. Die Arbeit wird weniger, und Sie können an Urlaub denken. Machen Sie eine große Reise und nehmen Sie einen netten Menschen mit!

> Denken Sie manchmal an Ihre Zukunft? Machen Sie *jetzt* neue Pläne und machen Sie im Beruf einmal etwas ganz anderes. Vorsicht: Ende Oktober wird es wahrscheinlich Probleme in Ihrer Familie geben, aber danach wird das Leben wieder ruhiger.

a. Is Ursula going to have a difficult time that month?

☐ yes

☐ no

Should Michael think about his future and change things?

☐ yes

☐ no

b. Is her work load going to be any easier from now on?

☐ yes

☐ no

Are there going to be a lot of problems at work at the end of October?

☐ yes

☐ no

c. Should she

☐ stay at home and work even harder

☐ go on holiday with someone nice?

When will life be quieter again?

☐ in October

☐ in November

Did you know?

Leisure time in West Germany

According to a survey a few years ago, over a third of the West Germans spent their Saturday night watching television. A further 25% said that they went to the pub, 7% had invited friends and 5% went to the theatre, the cinema or a concert.

Yet the Germans are not always as passive as that. They spend a lot of time and money on their hobbies, for example on do-it-yourself projects, photography, gardening and sports. The most popular sports are soccer, swimming, gymnastics, skiing and tennis. Even the smallest towns have their own outdoor (and often indoor) swimming pools, as well as a **Sportplatz** (sports field) for soccer and athletics. Jogging is becoming more and more popular, as a lot of Germans think increasingly about their health and fitness. In many towns you will find special fitness trails (**Trimm-dich-Pfade**). You jog along these trails, then you stop at certain points to do special exercises described on instruction boards.

Your turn to speak

1 Someone is asking you out for the evening. Answer his questions according to Michael's prompts. You'll practice:

Ich habe (keine) Lust
. . . mache ich nichts
Ja, gerne

2 You're talking to someone about holidays. You'll practice asking questions as well as giving answers, e.g.

Was für . . . haben Sie?
Wohin werden Sie fahren?
Was werden Sie machen?
Ich werde . . .

Revision/Review For the last revision section turn to p. 221.

Answers

Practice what you have learned p. 221 Exercise **1**(a) F (b) R (c) R
p. 211 Exercise **2** This is how you should have filled in the diary:

Freitag, 24. Juli	Samstag, 25. Juli	Sonntag, 26. Juli
bis 6 Uhr arbeiten, abends zu Hause, früh ins Bett	Sauna, Einkaufen, abends ins Kino	lange schlafen, lesen, spazieren gehen, abends Eltern besuchen

p. 212 Exercise **3**(b) im Sommer/drei Monate nach Sri Lanka
(c) Weihnachten/Eltern in Köln besuchen (d) Ostern/zu Hause bleiben
(e) heute nachmittag/mit den Kindern in den Zoo gehen

p. 212 Exercise **4**(a) yes (b) yes (c) Faust (d) modern (e) stay at home
(f) yes

Read and understand p. 214 (a) Ursula: no; Michael: yes (b) Ursula: yes;
Michael: no (c) Ursula: go on holiday with someone nice; Michael: in
November.

Revision/Review Units 1–3

At the end of every three chapters there will be special exercises on the cassette and here in the book to give you a chance to revise what you have learned so far. On this page you will find the revision exercises for Units 1–3. We suggest you proceed as follows:

1   Play through the dialogues from Units 1–3 again, reading them aloud from the book at the same time. (There are only a few minutes of dialogue in each unit, so this shouldn't take you too long).

2   Re-read the *Grammar* notes from each unit.

3   Make sure you know the *Key words and phrases* from each unit.

4   Do the revision exercises on tape which follow straight after Unit 3. You won't need your book for these exercises.

5   Do the written exercise below.

Exercise   Gudrun is staying at a hotel in Munich. She's writing a short note about her accommodation to her friend Emma who also lives in Munich. Read the note, then tick the right boxes below. (Answers p. 222)

Emma ,

Ich bin jetzt in München und wohne in einem Hotel im Stadtzentrum. Ich habe ein Einzelzimmer mit Balkon auf dem ersten Stock. Frühstück ist inklusiv. Ich möchte fünf Tage bleiben.

Viele Grüsse,

Gudrun

---

a. Where is Gudrun's room?

☐ on the ground floor

☐ on the first floor

b. What kind of room is it?

☐ a double room

☐ a single room

c. Has it got a balcony?

☐ yes

☐ no

d. Is breakfast included in the price?

☐ yes

☐ no

e. Where is the hotel?

☐ in the city centre

☐ in a suburb

f. How long does Gudrun want to stay?

☐ seven days

☐ five days

Revision/Review Units 4–6

In these units you have learned how to order snacks and drinks, to understand and ask for directions, and something about the time. Before going on to Unit 7, revise what you have learned in Units 4–6 as follows:

1 Listen to all the dialogues again.
2 Re-read the *Grammar* sections.
3 Test yourself on the *Key words and phrases*. Re-read them first, then cover up the German phrases and see whether you remember them from the English.
4 Make up exercises for yourself: Say the time aloud in German. Ask for the time. Order your favourite drink and/or snack. Ask for directions in your town. Practice the dates of your and your family's birthdays, your last/next holiday, etc.
5 Do the revision exercises on the cassette. They start straight after Unit 6.
6 Do the written exercises below.

Exercise 1

Here are some phrases you might hear or use in a restaurant or pub. Look back at the dialogues and the vocabulary as much as you need, then write the missing words in the boxes. The numbers 1–8 will give you the name of a month. Write it down below. (Answers p. 222)

a. Ist hier noch frei? – Nein, hier ist leider ⁵☐☐☐☐☐

b. Möchten Sie ein☐ ³☐☐☐Kuchen?

c. Möchten Sie Tee mit Milch oder mit ☐☐☐☐⁴☐☐?

d. Ein großes oder ein ²☐☐☐☐☐☐Bier?

e. Und was haben Sie auf der kalten ☐☐⁷☐☐?

f. Herr ¹☐☐☐☐zahlen bitte!

g. Getrennt oder☐☐☐☐☐⁶☐?

The name of the month is☐☐☐☐☐☐☐
                 1 2 3 4 5 6 7

Exercise 2

Study the answers given below, then write in the appropriate questions. (Answers p. 222)

a. .... Ja, wir fahren zum Museum.

b. .... Das ist die dritte Station.

c. .... Das kostet 1,50 DM

d. .... Es ist jetzt fünf nach drei.

Revision/Review Units 7-9

These units were concerned with shopping and travelling, and you had to cope with quite a lot of new vocabulary. Practice it a bit more before going on to Unit 10.

1 Revise the dialogues by listening to them and reading them aloud.
2 Re-read the *Grammar* notes and the *Key phrases*.
3 Re-read *Did you know?*
4 Test yourself: Describe the contents of your shopping basket in German. Make up a shopping list. Describe what you and your family are wearing. Ask for tickets to several destinations you might go to. Ask for the next train, plane, etc.
5 Do the tape exercises (after Unit 9).
6 Do the written exercises below.

Exercise 1   Have a look at the window display and the list of items next to it. Which of the items on this list are *not* on display in the window? (Answers p. 222)

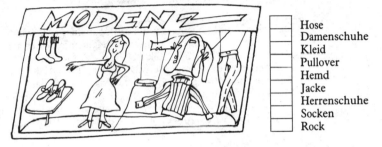

Hose
Damenschuhe
Kleid
Pullover
Hemd
Jacke
Herrenschuhe
Socken
Rock

Exercise 2   Study these signs, then answer the questions below. (Answers p. 222)

Information   SB Tank   Flughafen

Fahrkarten   Gleis   Autobahn

a. Which sign would you follow if you had a plane to catch?

....

b. Where would you enquire about trains? ....

c. Where would you board a train? ....

d. Where would you buy train tickets? ....

e. Where would you go for gas?   ....

f. Which sign would lead you to a motorway? ....

Revision/Review Units 10–12

Things are getting more complex – you've learned how to order a meal, how to say what you like and what you don't like, and how to describe your hometown and talk about the weather. Revise as follows:

1 Listen to all the dialogues once again.
2 Make sure you know the most important *Grammar* points and the *Key words and phrases*.
3 Test yourself by ordering your favorite food in German, stating your own likes and dislikes – e.g. what you like and don't like to eat and drink, where you like going on holiday etc. – , talk to someone (imaginary if necessary) about your hometown and the weather.
4 Do the tape exercises (after Unit 12).
5 Do the written exercise below.

Exercise Read what Wanda has to say about herself. Are the statements below True or False (**Richtig oder Falsch?**) (Answers p. 222)

> Ich heiße Wanda Niemeyer, bin aus München and wohne seit drei Jahren in Frankfurt. Frankfurt gefällt mir besser als München. Das Leben ist hektischer, die Atmosphäre ist liberaler, und es ist immer etwas los. Es gibt viele Kinos, Theater und Museen – und natürlich das Nachtleben! Frankfurt liegt am Main, und oft gehe ich nach der Arbeit am Fluß spazieren. Am Wochenende mache ich Wanderungen im Taunus. Das ist ein großer Wald in der Nähe von Frankfurt.

a. Wanda's home town is Munich. R F

b. She doesn't care much for Frankfurt. R F

c. Life in Frankfurt is quiet and subdued. R F

d. Frankfurt is also famous for its nightlife. R F

e. Frankfurt is situated by a lake. R F

f. Wanda goes for hiking tours on weekends. R F

Revision/Review Units 13–15

The last three units covered quite a lot of grammar. For example, the perfect, the imperfect and the future tenses were introduced. But remember that you do not have to *use* all these tenses. Concentrate on the perfect which is the most important tense if you want to talk about the past.

Revise as follows:
1 Listen again to all the dialogues in these units.
2 Re-read all the *Grammar* sections carefully, especially in Unit 13 where the perfect tense is explained.
3 Revise the *Key phrases* thoroughly.
4 Ask yourself **Was habe ich gestern gemacht?** (What did I do yesterday?) and **Was mache ich morgen?** (What am I doing tomorrow?) and jot down some answers.
5 Do the tape exercises (after Unit 15).
6 Do the written exercise below.

Exercise

Have a look at the drawings. Then complete the captions by picking the right words from the list below. (Answers p. 222)

a. Ich habe bis 7 Uhr ....

b. Du hast mich zu spät ....

....

c. Ich bin mit dem Bus in die

Stadt ....

d. Mittags haben wir im

Restaurant ....

e. Dann ....

wir eine Konferenz

f. Abends haben wir unsere

Freunde ....

| geweckt | besucht | gefahren | gegessen |
| hatten | | geschlafen | |

Revision/Review answers

Units 1–3 p. 217 (**a**) on the first floor (**b**) a single room (**c**) yes (**d**) yes
(**e**) in the city centre (**f**) five days

Units 4–6 p. 218 Exercise **1(a)** BES<u>E</u>TZT (**b**) ST<u>Ü</u>CK (**c**) ZITR<u>O</u>NE
(**d**) <u>K</u>LEINES (**c**) KA<u>R</u>TE (**f**) <u>O</u>BER (**g**) ZUS<u>A</u>MM<u>E</u>N = **OKT<u>O</u>BER**

p. 218 Exercise **2(a)** Fahren Sie zum Museum? (**b**) Welche Station ist das?
(**c**) Was kostet das? (**d**) Wie spät ist es?

Units 7–9 p. 219 Exercise **1** The items *not* on display are **Herrenschuhe**
(men's shoes) and **Hemd** (shirt)

p. 219 Exercise **2(a)** Flughafen (**b**) Information (**c**) Gleis 12a
(**d**) Fahrkarten (**e**) SB Tank (**f**) Autobahn

Units 10–12 p. 220 (**a**) R (**b**) F (**c**) F (**d**) R (**e**) F (**f**) R

Units 13–15 p. 221 (**a**) geschlafen (**b**) geweckt (**c**) gefahren (**d**) gegessen
(**e**) hatten (**f**) besucht

Grammar summary

Below you will find a short summary of what we think are the most important grammar points occurring in this course. Some useful grammar terms will also be explained.

VERBS infinitive	A verb is a word denoting action or being, e.g. I *am*, he *goes*, she *loves* him. The simplest form of the verb is called *infinitive*. In English this form is preceded by 'to': to love, to go, to be, etc. In German all verbs in the infinitive end in **-en** or **-n**, e.g. **gehen** (to go), **tun** (to do). These infinitive endings change according to the subject of the verb, i.e. who or what acts: **ich gehe** (I go), **du gehst** (you go), **wir gehen** (we go), etc. In the present tense (see 'tenses' below) these endings are the same for most verbs
stem	(see Unit 2 p. 31), but sometimes the vowel in the *stem*, or main part of the verb, changes in the **du, er, sie** and **es** forms, e.g. **sprechen** (to speak): **du sprichst, er/sie/es spricht; fahren** (to go, to drive): **du fährst, er/sie/es fährt.**
strong verbs	These verbs are called *strong verbs.*
Use of verbs	Remember that in English there are two ways of expressing an action, e.g. 'I eat' and 'I am eating'. In German there is only one: **ich esse.** This applies to all tenses.
tenses	A tense says *when* you are doing something, e.g. now (in the *present*), some time ago (in the *past* or at some point sooner or later (in the *future*).
perfect	There are two ways of talking about the past in German: the *perfect* tense and the *imperfect* tense. The perfect tense is explained in Unit 13 p. 185. It is more widely used than the imperfect, so it is more important for you to learn. The perfect is formed with the present of **haben** or **sein: ich habe gewohnt, ich bin gereist.** (I have lived, I have travelled). **Gereist** and **gewohnt** are the *past participles* of the verbs **reisen** and **wohnen**. Remember that the participles of regular verbs are formed by putting **ge-** in front and **-t** after the stem: **gereist, gewohnt,** but that there are also irregular forms: **ich bin gekommen** (I have come), **ich habe unterrichtet** (I have taught).
imperfect	The *imperfect* is used to describe actions which happened quite a long time ago, e.g. **vor 10 Jahren wohnte er in Ulm** (10 years ago he lived in Ulm). Regular verbs form their imperfect by inserting **-t** after the stem: **ich wohnte, du wohntest,** etc. (see Unit 14 p. 199).
strong verbs	Strong verbs, e.g. **fahren: ich fuhr, du fuhrst, er/sie/es/fuhr, wir fuhren, ihr fuhrt, sie fuhren.** Instead of inserting **-t** these verbs change their stem altogether. Note that closely related English verbs often do the same, e.g. **singen sang gesungen** (sing, sang, sung) **trinken trank getrunken** (drink, drank, drunk). Dictionaries will list all strong verbs.
Use of the past tenses	Remember that the perfect in German often has to be the imperfect in English (see Unit 13 p. 185): **Gestern habe ich bis elf Uhr geschlafen.** Yesterday I *slept* till eleven o'clock.
future	The future is formed in German with the present of **werden** and the infinitive of the verb: **ich werde gehen, du wirst gehen,** etc. (I'll go, you'll go, etc.) (see Unit 15 p. 213). In German you can often use the present tense to state future intentions: **Morgen fahre ich nach Hause.** Tomorrow I'll go home.
modal verbs	Modal verbs are verbs like **müssen** (must), **können** (can), **dürfen** (may), **wollen** (to want to), **sollen** (shall, ought to), **möchten** (to like to do s.th.) They are explained in Unit 9 p. 129
separable verbs	These are verbs like **anfangen** (to begin), **zumachen** (to shut), **aufhören** (to stop), etc. They consist of two parts, a short *prefix* (like **an, auf, zu,** etc.) and then a verb. In the infinitive these two parts appear together, but otherwise they are split up: **ich fange an** (I begin), **wir machen zu** (we shut). In longer sentences the prefix goes right to the end: **Wir fangen um neun Uhr an.** (We start at nine) **Wir hören um 12 Uhr auf.** (We stop at 12) *Note:* If there is also a modal verb, the separable verb is joined up again, e.g. **ich möchte aufhören** (I want to stop), **wir wollen jetzt anfangen** (we want to start now). (See also Unit 6 p. 81).

NOUNS	A noun is the name of a person or thing, e.g. *James, dog, book, fun.* In German all nouns have a capital initial letter: **da ist ein <u>Mann</u>** (there's a man); **siehst du die <u>Frau</u>?** (do you see the woman?)
genders	All German nouns are either masculine, feminine or neuter, e.g. they have a *gender*. You can tell the gender of a noun when it is used with the words for 'the' (**der/die/das**) and 'a' (**ein/eine/ein**).
articles	These words are called *articles*: masc. **der/ein Mann** the/a man fem. **die/eine Frau** the/a woman neut. **das/ein Kind** the/a child In German the articles often undergo changes according to the function a noun has in a sentence. It can, for example, be the *subject* or the *object*. A subject is a person or thing
subject	who acts, e.g.
object	*'the woman* is reading'. The object is the person or thing on the receiving end, e.g. 'the woman reads *the paper*'. Whereas in English 'the' or 'a' is used regardless of whether a noun is a subject or an object, the articles often change in German when a noun becomes an object, i.e. when its function or *case* is changed. (see Unit 3 p. 45).
cases	There are four cases altogether. In this course you have met three:[1] **1.** the *nominative* (when a noun is the subject) e.g. *the man* is here. **2.** the *accusative* (when a noun is the direct object) e.g. I see *the man.* **3.** the *dative* (when a noun is the indirect object) e.g. I give the book *to the man.* Here are the nominative, accusative and dative forms for **der/die/das:**

	singular			plural
	masc.	fem.	neut.	all genders
nom.	**der Mann**	**die Frau**	**das Kind**	**die Männer/Frauen/Kinder**
acc.	**de<u>n</u> Mann**	**die Frau**	**das Kind**	**die Männer/Frauen/Kinder**
dat.	**de<u>m</u> Mann**	**de<u>r</u> Frau**	**de<u>m</u> Kind**	**de<u>n</u> Männer<u>n</u>/Frauen/Kinder<u>n</u>**

Ein/eine/ein

	masc.	fem.	neut.
nom.	**ein Mann**	**eine Frau**	**ein Kind**
acc.	**eine<u>n</u> Mann**	**eine Frau**	**ein Kind**
dat.	**eine<u>m</u> Mann**	**eine<u>r</u> Frau**	**eine<u>m</u> Kind**

The negative of ein/eine/ein is **kein/keine/kein** (no, none) and follows the same pattern. So do **mein** (my), **dein** (your) and **sein** (his).

PRONOUNS	Pronounds stand for a noun, e.g. *Mary* loves *Fred – she* loves *him*. In German there are nominative, accusative and dative pronounds.

nom.		acc.		dat.	
ich	I	**mich**	me	**mir**	(to) me
du	you	**dich**	you	**dir**	(to) you
er	he	**ihn**	him	**ihm**	(to) him
sie	she	**sie**	her	**ihr**	(to) her
es	it	**es**	it	**ihm**	(to) it
wir	we	**uns**	us	**uns**	(to) us
ihr	you	**euch**	you	**euch**	(to) you
Sie	you	**Sie**	you	**Ihnen**	(to) you
sie	they	**sie**	them	**ihnen**	(to) them

Note that the dative is often translated by *to + pronoun* in English, e.g.
Er gab es mir.   **Wir sagten es ihm.**
He gave it *to me.*   We said it *to him.*
Often you will find the dative form of pronouns in phrases like **es gefällt mir, es schmeckt Ihnen, wie geht es dir?** etc.

---

[1] The fourth case is called the *genitive* which didn't come up in this course.

PREPOSITIONS	Prepositions are words like near, by, in, to, through, over, etc. (see Unit 5 p. 73). In German certain prepositions take certain cases, e.g. **aus** (out of, form) takes the dative: **Er kommt aus dem Norden.** He comes from the north. And **durch** (through) takes the accusative: **Wir gehen durch den Garten.** We go through the garden.
prepositions with the dative	Prepositions which *only* take the dative:

von (from, of)	**aus** (out of, from)
zu (to, at)	**seit** (since, for)
nach (to, after)	**mit** (with)
bei (at)	**gegenüber** (opposite) **außer** (except)

prepositions with the accusative	Prepositions which take the accusative only:

durch (through)	**gegen** (against, towards)
entlang (along)	**ohne** (without)
für (for)	**um** (around, at)

prepositions with dative or accusative	Prepositions which take the dative *or* the accusative:

in (in, into)	**neben** (next to)
an (on, to, at)	**zwischen** (between)
auf (on, on to)	**über** (over, across)
vor (in front of, ago)	**unter** (under, below)
hinter (behind)	

	With these preopositions the accusative is used if there is *movement* to a place: **Er ging** in *den* Garten. He went into the garden.
	The dative is used if there is *no* movement: **Er stand** im (= in dem) **Garten.** He was standing in the garden.
ADJECTIVES comparisons	Adjectives are words like 'good', 'bad', 'red', 'pretty' etc. (see Units 7 and 8 pp. 101 and 115). You use adjectives if you want to describe and compare things, e.g. **Das Kind ist groß.** The child is tall. **Die Frau ist größer.** The woman is taller. **Der Mann ist am größten.** The man is tallest. Be aware of the fact that adjectives, like articles, change if they are in front of the noun in certain cases, e.g.

singular:	masc.	fem.	neut.	plural (all genders)
nom.	der kleine Mann	die kleine Frau	das kleine Kind	die kleinen Männer
acc.	den kleinen Mann	die kleine Frau	das kleine Kind	die kleinen Männer
dat.	dem kleinen Mann	der kleinen Frau	dem kleinen Kind	den kleinen Männern
nom.	ein kleiner Mann	eine kleine Frau	ein kleines Kind	kleine Männer
acc.	einen kleinen Mann	eine kleine Frau	ein kleines Kind	kleine Männer
dat.	einem kleinen Mann	einer kleinen Frau	einem kleinen Kind	kleinen Männern

Vocabulary

The *plural* of nouns is given in brackets, e.g.
Akademiker (–) no change in plural: **Akademiker**
Abend(e) add **e**: **Abende**
Anfang (¨e) add **e** and stem vowel takes *Umlaut:* **Anfänge**
Mutter (¨) no change except for *Umlaut* in stem vowel: **Mütter**
Bank(en) add **en**: **Banken**
Brücke(n) add **n**: **Brücken**
Dorf(¨er) add **er** and vowel takes *Umlaut:* **Dörfer**
Anschluß (¨sse) add **e**, put *Umlaut* on vowel and modify ß to **ss**:
  Anschlüsse
Genie(s) add **s**: **Genies**
Datum (Daten) irregular plural
If nothing is given in brackets, there is no plural for that particular word,
or the plural is hardly ever used:
Benzin petrol
If **(pl.)** appears in brackets, the word is used in the plural only:
Leute (pl.) people.

The *gender* of nouns is given after the brackets: **m.** means *masculine,* **f.**
feminine and **n.** *neuter* nouns:

Besuch(e) m. visit
Dame (n) f. lady
Haus(¨er) n. house

ab off, away
ab departing; **ab Ulm 14.05**
  departing Ulm 14.05
ab und zu every now and then
Abend(e), m. evening; **abends** in
  the evening
Abendessen (–) n. supper
aber but
abfahren to depart
Abfahrt(en), f. departure
abwaschen to wash up
acht eight
Achtel (–), n. one eighth
Adler (–), m. eagle
Adria, f. Adriatic coast
Aha! (exclamation) I see!
Akademiker (–), m. person with
  academic qualifications
akademisch academic
alles all, everything; **alles
  Gute** all the best
allein(e) alone
(die) Alpen the Alps
also that is (to say)
alt old; **alter Knabe** (colloquial)
  old fellow
Altbau(ten), m. old building

Altbauwohnung, (en) f. flat in an
  old house
Altstadt(¨e), f. old part of town
am (an + dem) at; **am
  Bahnhof** at the station; **am
  besten** best
Ampel(n), f. traffic light
amüsant amusing
an at
an arriving; **Ulm an 13.05**
  arriving Ulm 13.05
an sich actually
andere other; **die andern** the
  others
Anfang(¨e), m. beginning
anfangen to begin, to start
angenehm pleasant
Angestellte(n), m.f. employee
ankommen to arrive
Ankunft(¨e), f. arrival
Anschluß(¨sse) m. connection
Ansichtskarte(n) f. picture postcard
Apfel (¨), m. apple
Appetit, m. appetite; **guten
  Appetit** enjoy your meal
April m. April
Arbeit(en), f. work

arbeiten to work
Art(en), f. species, kind
Aschenbecher (–), m. ashtray
auch also as well, too
auf on, in;   auf dem 1. Stock on
the 1st floor;   auf englisch in
English
auf open
aufhaben to be open
aufhören to stop
aufmachen to open
aufpassen to be careful, to look
after
aufräumen to tidy up
Aufschnitt, m. selection of cheeses
(Käseaufschnitt) or sausages
(Wurstaufschnitt)
aufstehen to get up
August, m. August
aus from out of
Ausfahrt(en), f. exit
Auskunft(¨e) f, information
Ausland n. foreign country;
im Ausland abroad
außer except
Ausstellung(en) f. exhibition.
Ausstieg(e), m. exit (in trams,
buses or trains)
Autobahn(en), f. motorway
Atmosphäre(n), f. atmosphere

Bad(¨er), n. bath
Bäckerei(en), f. bakery
Bahn(en), f. train
Bahnhof(¨e), m. station
Balkon(e), m. balcony
Banane(n), f. banana
Bank(en), f. bank
Bar(s), f. bar
Bär(en), m. bear
Bauernhof(¨e), m. farm
Baumwolle f. cotton
Bayern n. Bavaria
bayrisch Bavarian
bedeckt overcast
begeistert enthusiastic, thrilled
bei near, at
beide both
Beilage(n), f. side dish
Beispiel(e), n. example; z.B. =
zum Beispiel for example
Beitz(en), f. (colloquial) pub
bekannt famous
bekommen to get
belegte Brote sandwiches
beliebt popular
Benzin n. petrol
bereits already

Berg(e), m. mountain
Berghütte(n), f. mountain cabin
Bergkristall(e) n. rock crystal
Beruf(e), m. profession von
Beruf by profession
berühmt famous
besetzt taken, occupied; hier ist
leider besetzt I'm afraid this seat
is taken
besichtigen to visit, to have a
look at
besonders especially
besser better
beste, r, s best
bestimmt certainly
Besuch(e), m. visit
besuchen to visit, to go and see
bewölkt cloudy
bezahlen to pay
Bier(e), n. beer
bieten to offer
Bild(er), n. picture, painting
Birne(n), f. pear
bis until, till; bis jetzt so far; bis
dann till then
(ein) bißchen a bit, a little
bitte please, you're welcome, beg
your pardon
bitter bitter
blau blue
bleiben to stay
Blick(e), m. view
bloß only
Blumenkohl(e), m. cauliflower
Bluse(n), f. blouse
Blut n. blood
Bodensee m. Lake Constance
Bootsfahrt(en), f. boat trip
Bouillon(s), n. clear broth
Braten(–), m. roast
braten to fry
Brathähnchen(–), n. roast chicken
Bratwurst(¨e)f. fried/grilled sausage
Brauerei(en), f. brewery
braun brown
BRD f. (Bundersrepublik
Deutschland) Federal Republic
of Germany
breit broad
Brief(e), m. letter
Briefmarke(n), f. stamp
bringen to take, bring
Brot(e), n. bread
Brötchen(–), n. roll
Brücke(n), f. bridge
Buch(¨er), book
buchen to book
Butter f. butter

Campingplatz(¨e), m. campsite
Creme f. cream

da because, there, then
dahin (to) there
Dame(n), f. lady
damit so that
danach after that
danke (schön) thank you (very much) **vielen Dank** many thanks
danken to thank
dann then
darf: was darf's sein? can I help you? (see also **dürfen**)
das the (neuter nouns), that, this
Datum (Daten), n. date
dauern to take (time); **wie lange dauert es?** how long does it take?
dazu with it
DDR, f. (**Deutsche Demokratische Republik**) German Democratic Republic
denken to think, to believe
der the (m).
deutsch German
Deutschland n. Germany
Dezember(–) m. December
dick fat
die the (f)
Dienstag(e), m. Tuesday
dies this; **dies ist** this is
diese, r, s this
Ding(e), n. thing; **vor allen Dingen** above all things
Diskothek(en), f. discotheque
Donnerstag(e), Thursday
Doppelzimmer(–), n. double room
Dorf(¨er), n. village
dort there
dorthin (to) there
draußen outside, outdoors
drei three
dritte, r,s third
drüben: da drüben over there
du you (familiar address, sing.)
durch through
dürfen may, to be allowed to
Dusche(n), f. shower
D-Zug(¨e), m. express train

ebenfalls also
Ei(er), n. egg
eigentlich in fact, really, actually
eilig in a hurry
Eilzug(¨e) fast train
einfach simple; one-way (ticket); **nach Ulm einfach** a one-way to Ulm

einmal once, one; **einmal Ulm einfach** one one-way (ticket) to Ulm
ein,e a; **ein Mann** a man; **eine Frau** a woman
eins one
einsteigen to board
Einwohner(–), m. inhabitant
Einzelfahrschein(e), m. single ticket
einzeln single
Eis n. ice, ice cream
elegant elegant
elf eleven
Elfenbein n. ivory
empfehlen to recommend
Endstation(en), f. terminus
England n. England
Engländer(–), m. Englishman
Engländerin(nen), f. Englishwoman; **ich bin Engländer(in)** I am English
englisch English
Entdeckung(en), f. discovery
entfernt distant, away
entschuldigen to excuse; **entschuldigen Sie bitte** excuse me please
Entschuldigung(en), f. excuse
Entwerter (–), m. ticket canceller machine
er he
Erdbeere(n), f. strawberry
(sich) erholen to rest, to relax
erreichen to reach
erst at first
erste, r, s first
erwarten to expect
es it
essen to eat
Etage(n), f. floor
etwas some, a little, something
Europa n. Europe
europäisch European

fahren to go (by bus, tram, train), to drive
Fahrer(–), m. driver
Fahrgast(¨e), m. passenger
Fahrkarte(n), f. ticket
Fahrschein(e), m. ticket
Fahrzeit(en), f. length of journey
Familie(n), f. family
fangen to catch
Farbe(n), f. colour
fast nearly, almost
faulenzen to laze about
Februar m. February

Feld(er), n. field
Ferien (pl.) holidays
Ferienhaus(¨er) holiday house, n.
Ferienwohnung(en), f. holiday flat
Ferne Osten m. the Far East
Ferngespräch(e), n. long distance
  telephone call
Fernsehen, n. television
fernsehen to watch TV
finden to find
Firma (Firmen), f. firm
Fisch(e), m. fish
fischen to fish
fit fit
Flasche(n), f. bottle
Fleisch n. meat
fliegen to fly
Flug(¨e), m. flight
Flughafen ("–), m. airport
Flugschein(e), m. airticket
Flugzeit(en), f. flying time
Flugzeug(e), n. plane
Fluß(¨sse), m. river
Forelle(n), f. trout
Frage(n), f. question
fragen to ask
Frankreich n. France
französisch French
Frau(en), f. wife, woman, Mrs
Fräulein (–), n. Miss
frei free
freiberuflich freelance
Freitag(e), m. Friday
Freizeit f. spare time
Fremdenverkehrsamt(¨er), n.
  tourist office
Freund(e), m. friend, m.;
Freundin(nen), f. friend, f.
freundlich friendly
frisch fresh
Friseur(e), m. hairdresser
Frost(¨e) m. frost
Frucht(¨e), f. fruit
Fruchtsaft(¨e), m. fruit juice
Frühjahr n. spring
Frühstück n. breakfast
fünf five
für for
Fuß(¨e) m. foot; zu Fuß on foot
Fußball m. football
Fußgängerzone(n), f. pedestrian
  mall

ganz quite, whole; ganz
  durch straight through
Gasse(n), f. alleyway
Gast(¨), m. guest
Gasthof(¨e) m. inn

Gaststätte(n), f. inn, pub
Gastwirtschaft(en), f. pub
geben to give
gebietsweise in places
gefallen to please; es gefällt
  mir I like it
gegen against, round about; gegen
  7 Uhr round about seven
gehen to go, to walk; wie geht es
  Ihnen? how are you?
gelb yellow
Geld(er), n. money
Geldwechsel(–), m. exchange
  (money)
gemeinsam together
gemischt mixed
Gemüse(–) n. vegetable
genial ingenious
Genie(s), n. genius
geöffnet open(ed)
Gepäck n. luggage
Gepäckaufbewahrung f. left
  luggage
geradeaus straight on
Gerät(e), n. tool, gadget
Gericht(e), n. dish
gering few
gern with pleasure
Geschäft(e), n. business, shop
Geschäftsreise(n), f. business trip
Geschenk(e), n. present
geschieden divorced
geschlossen shut
getrennt separately
Getränk(e), n. drink
gewiß certainly
Gewitter(–), n. thunderstorm
gewittrig thundery
Glas(¨er) n. glass
Glatteis n. ice patch
glauben to believe, to think
gleich immediately, equal
Gleis(e), n. platform, track
Glück n. luck, happiness
glücklich happy
Gott(¨er), m. god; Gott sei
  Dank thank God
Grapefruit(s), f. grapefruit
Grenze(n), f. border
Griechenland n. Greece
griechisch Greek
groß big; im großen und
  ganzen on the whole
Großstadt(¨e) f. big city
Größe(n), f. size
größer bigger
grün green
Gruppe(n), f. group

Gruß(¨e), m. greeting; **viele Grüße** many greetings
grüßen to greet
Grüß Gott hello (South German, Swiss, Austrian)
Gold n. gold
golden golden
Gulasch m. goulash
günstig reasonable (price)
Gurke(n), f. cucumber
gut good; **guten Tag/Morgen/ Abend** good day/morning/ evening; **gute Nacht** good-night
Gymnasium (Gymnasien), n. grammar school

Haar(e), n. hair
haben to have
halb half
Hals(¨e), m. throat, neck
halten to stop, to keep
Haltestelle(n), f. stop
hassen to hate
Hauptbahnhof(¨e), m. main station
Hauptspeise(n), f. main dish
Haupstraße(n), f. main street, high street
Haus(¨er), n. house
Hausarbeit, f. housework
Häuschen(–), n. little house
Hausfrau(en), f. housewife
Hausmann(¨er), m. house husband
hätte would have; **was hätten Sie gern?** what would you like to have?
Hausmannskost f. home cooking
heiß hot (temperature)
heißen to be called; **ich heiße Anton** my name is Anton
heiter bright, fair
Hektik, f. frenzy
hektisch hectic
helfen to help
Hemd(en), n. shirt
herb dry (of wines)
Herbst m. autumn
Herr(en), m. Mr, gentleman
heute today; **heute morgen** this morning; **heute abend** this evening
hier hier
hin und her to and fro
hin und zurück return, there and back
hinter behind
hinüber over
hinunter down
historisch historical

Hobby(s), n. hobby
Hochhaus(¨er), n. high rise building
Höchsttemperatur(en), f. maximum temperature
hoffen to hope
Höhe(n), f. altitude, height
holen to fetch
Honig m. honey
Hose(n), f. (pair of) trousers
Hotelführer(–), m. hotel guide (book)

ich I
ideal ideal
ihr you (familiar address, pl.)
Imbiß (sse), m. snack
Imbißstube(n), f. snack bar
immer always
Indien n. India
Industrie(n), f. industry
Information(en), f. information
Ingenieur(e), m. engineer
inklusiv inclusive(ly)
Inland n. within a country; **im Inland** at home
Insektenstich(e), m. insect bite
Insel(n), f. island
(sich) interessieren(für) to be interested in
international international
intim intimate
Italien n. Italy
italienisch Italian

ja yes
Jacke(n), f. jacket, cardigan
Jackett(s), n. (men's) jacket
Jahr(e), n. year
Jahrhundert(e), n. century
Januar m. January
jawohl yes, indeed! certainly!
jede, r, s each, every
jetzt now
Joghurt(e), m. yoghurt
Jugendherberge(n), f. youth hostel
Jugendliche (–), m., f. youth
Jugoslawien n. Jugoslavia
Juli m. July
Junge(n), m. boy
Juni m. June

Kaffee m. coffee
Kaiser(–), m. emperor
Kakao m. cocoa
Kalb (¨er), n. calf, veal
kalt cold
kalte Karte snack menu

Kännchen (–), n. small pot, jug
Kanne(n), f. (tea, coffee) pot
Karotte (n), f. carrot
Karte(n), f. card, ticket, menu
Käse m. cheese
Käsesahnetorte(n), f. rich cheese gâteau
Kasse(n), f. cash desk
kaum scarcely
kegeln to play skittles
kein, e no, none; **kein Kind** no child; **keiner** nobody
Kenntnis(se), f. knowledge
Kind(er), n. child
Kinder(fahr)karte(n), f. children's ticket
Kindheit f. childhood
Kino(s), n. cinema
Kiosk(e), m. kiosk
Kirche(n), f. church
Kirsche(n), f. cherry
klappen to work out; **es klappt gut** it works well
klar clear
Klasse(n), f. class
Klavier(e), n. piano
Klee m. clover
Kleid(er), n. dress
klein small
Kleinstadt("e), f. small town
kleinstädtisch provincial
klingen to sound
Klub(s), m. club
Kneipe(n), f. (colloquial) pub
Knödel(–), m. dumpling
kochen to cook
Kollege(n), m. colleague, m. **Kollegin (nen)**, f. colleague, f.
komisch comical, funny
kommen to come
Konditorei(en), f. patisserie
König(e), m. king
können can, to be able to; **könnte** could
Konzert(e), n. concert
Kopf("e), m. head
Kopfsalat(e), m. lettuce salad
Kopfschmerz(en), m. headache; **ich habe Kopfschmerzen** I've got a headache
kosten to cost
Kotelett(s), n. cutlet, chop
kräftig strong, bright (colours)
krank ill
Kuchen(–), m. cake
kühl cool
kultiviert cultured
Kultur(en), f. culture

kulturell cultural
Kurs(e), m. exchange rate

Lage(n), f. location, situation
Lamm("er), n. lamb
Land("er), n. land, country; **auf dem Land** in the country
landen to land
Landschaft(en), f. countryside, scenery, landscape
Landung(en), f. landing
langsam slow(ly)
langweilig boring
Lärm m. noise
laufen to run; **wir laufen** we'll walk
laut loud, noisy
leben to live
Lebensmittelgeschäft(e), n. food shop
Leberwurst("e), f. liver sausage
ledig single
Lehrer(–), m. teacher
leicht light
leid: es tut mir leid I'm sorry
leider unfortunately
lesen to read
Leute (pl.) people
lieben to love
lieber preferably; **ich nehme lieber Tee** I'd rather have tea
liegen to lie
Liegewagen(–), m. couchette
Linie(n), f. tramline, bus route; **schlanke Linie** slimline
links left
Lokal(e), n. pub
Lotion(en), f. lotion
Luftpost f. airmail
Lust f. (lit.) lust; **hast du Lust?** do you feel like. . .?
lustig jolly
lutschen to suck

machen to do, to make
Mädchen(–), n. girl
mager lean, skimmed (milk)
Mai m. May
Mal(e), n. time(s); **ein anderes Mal** another time; **dreimal** three times
malen to paint
man one; **man kann das nicht machen** one can't do that
manchmal sometimes
Mann("er), m. man, husband
Mantel(–), m. coat
Markt("e), m. market

Marmelade (n), f. jam, marmalade
März m. March
Maschine(n), f. engine, plane
mäßig moderate
Mehl n. flour
Mehrfahrtenkarte(n), f. ticket for several trips
meine my
meistens in most cases
Mensch(en), m. man
Menschheit f. mankind
Messe(n), f. trade fair
Metzgerei(en), f. butcher's
mieten to rent, to hire
Milch, f. milk
mild mild
Minute(n), f. minute
mit with
mitgehen to come along, to go along
Mittagessen(–), n. lunch
Mittel(–), n. remedy, means
mittlere medium
Mittwoch m. Wednesday
möchten to like (to do); **ich möchte gerne** I'd very much like
Moment(e), m. moment; **im Moment** at the moment
Monat(e), m. month
Montag m. Monday
Morgen(–), m. morning
morgen tomorrow; **morgen abend** tomorrow evening
morgen früh early tomorrow
morgens in the morning
Mosel, f. Moselle river
Mosel, m. Moselle wine
Motiv(e), n. motif
Mund("er), m. mouth
Museum (Museen), n. museum
Musikhochschule(n), f. academy of music
müssen must, to have to

nach to, after; **nach London** to London; **nach 6** after 6
Nachmittag(e), m. afternoon
nachmittags in the afternoon
nächste, r, s next, nearest; **der nächste Zug** the next train; **die nächste Bank** the nearest bank
Nacht("e), f. night
Nachtleben n. nightlife
nachts at night
Nähe f. proximity; **in der Nähe von** near

Name(n), m. name
naß wet
Nebel (–), m. fog
Nebelfeld("er), n. foggy patch
neben next to
neblig foggy
nee (colloquial) no
nehmen to take
nein no
nennen to mention, to name
nett nice
neu new
Neubau(ten), m. new building
neun nine
nicht not; **nicht wahr?** isn't that true?
nie never
Niederschlag("e), m. rainfall
niederschlagsfrei free of rainfall
Nobelpreis(e), m. Nobel prize
noch still, as yet; **noch nicht** not yet
Norden m. north
nördlich north
normal normal
November m. November
Nudel(n), f. noodle

oben above, on top
Ober(–), m. waiter; **Herr Ober!** waiter!
Ochse(n), m. ox
Ochsenmaulsalat(e), m. ox muzzle salad
oder or
offen open
Öffnungszeit(en), f. opening hour
Oh je! (exclamation) oh dear!
ohne without
Oktober m. October
Öl m. oil
Orange(n), f. orange
Ort(e), m. town, place
örtlich in places
Osten m. east
Ostern Easter
Österreich n. Austria
österreichisch Austrian

Paar(e), n. pair
Packung(en), f. packet
Park(s), m. park
Parkplatz("e), m. parking space, car park
Parterre ground floor; **im Parterre** on the ground floor
passen to fit
passieren to happen

Patentamt (¨er), n. patent office
Patrizier(–), m. patrician
Pause(n), f. break
Pension(en), f. boarding house
perfekt perfect
Persönlichkeit(en), f. personality
Pfirsich(e), m. peach
Pfund(e), n. pound
Pinte(n), f. (colloquial) pub
Plakat(e), n. poster
Plan(¨e), m. plan
planen to plan; **planmäßige**
  Abfahrt scheduled departure
Platz(¨e), m. square, seat, place
Platzkarte(n), f. seat reservation
Pommes frites (pl.) French fries
Portugal n. Portugal
Post f. post office, mail
Postbeamte(n), m. post office
  official
Posten(–), m. post
Postkarte(n), f. postcard
Präparat(e), n. medication;
  medicine
Preis(e), m. price, prize
Preislage(n), f. price range
preiswert good value, reasonable
Prestige n. prestige
prima great, super
Probe(n), f. trial test
probieren to try (out);
  anprobieren to try on (clothes)
Professor(en), m. professor, m.
Professorin(nen), f. professor, f.
Prospekt(e), m. prospectus,
  brochure
Pullover(–), m. pullover, sweater

Querstraße(n), f. crossroads
Rathaus(¨er), n. town hall
rauchen to smoke
rechts (to the) right
Regen m. rain
reif mature
Reis m. rice
Reise(n), f. journey; **gute**
  Reise have a good journey
reisen to travel
Rentner(–), m. pensioner, m.
Rentnerin(nen), f. pensioner, f.
reservieren to reserve
richtig (that's) right
Richtung(en), f. direction; **in**
  Richtung Ulm in the direction of
  Ulm
Rind(er), n. beef, cattle
Rindfleisch n. beef
Rippchen(–), n. sparerib

Rock(¨e), m. skirt
roh raw, fresh
rot red
Rotwein(e), m. red wine
Rückfahrkarte(n), f. return ticket
ruhen to rest
Ruhetag(e), m. day off
ruhig quiet
rund round
rundum all round
Russische Eier (lit. Russian eggs)
  eggs mayonnaise

Saft(¨e), m. juice
sagen to say, to tell
Sahne f. cream
Salami f. salami
Salat(e), m. salad, lettuce
Salatplatte(n), f. salad platter
Salz(e), n. salt
salzig salty
Salzkartoffeln potatoes boiled in
  saltwater
Sammelkarte(n), f. ticket for
  several trips
sammeln to collect
Samstag m. Saturday
Sandale(n), f. sandal
S-Bahn(en), f. commuter train
scharf sharp, hot (spicy)
Schauer(–), m. shower
Scheck(s), m. cheque
Scheibe(n), f. slice;
  Fensterscheibe(n), f. window
  pane
Schein(e), m. (bank) note
schick chique
Schinken(–), m. ham
schlafen to sleep
Schlafwagen(–), m. sleeper
schlank slim
schlecht bad
schließen to shut
Schließfach(¨er), n. luggage locker
schlucken to swallow
Schlüssel(–), m. key
schmecken to taste; **schmeckt es**
  Ihnen? are you enjoying your
  food?
Schmerz(en), m. pain, ache
Schmuck, m. jewellery
Schnee m. snow
Schneider(–), m. tailor
schnell quick
Schnellimbiß(sse) m. snack bar
Schnellzug(¨e), m. fast train
Schnitzel n. slice of pork or veal
Schokolade(n), f. chocolate

schon already
schön beautiful
schreiben to write
Schuh(e), m. shoe
Schule(n), f. school
Schwaben n. Swabia
schwäbisch Swabian
schwach light, weak
schwarz black
Schwarzwald m. Black Forest
Schwein(e), n. pig, pork
Schweinebraten(–), m. roast pork
Schweinshaxe(n), f. pig's knuckle
(die) Schweiz f. Switzerland
schwer difficult, heavy
schwierig difficult
schwimmen to swim
sechs six
See(n), m. lake
sehen to see
Sehenswürdigkeit(en), f. sight
sehr very
sein to be
seit since, for **seit 14 Jahren** for
   14 years; **seit November** since
   November
Seite(n), f. side, page
Sekt m. sparkling wine
Sekunde(n), f. second
Selbstbedienung f. self service
selbsttätig automatically
selbstverständlich of course
selten seldom
September m. September
Serbisches Reisfleisch Serbian
   meat and rice dish
Serie(n), f. series
sie she, they
Sie you (polite form of address,
   sing. and pl.)
sieben seven
Silber n. silver
skifahren, skilaufen to ski
Skigebiet(e), n. skiing area/resort
Socke(n), f. sock
sogar even
Sohn(¨e), m. son
sollen shall, ought to;
   soll ich? shall I?
Sommer(–), m. summer
sommerlich summery
Sonderangebot(e), n. special offer
Sonderfahrkarte(n), f. special
   ticket
Sonne(n), f. sun
sonnig sunny
Sonntag m. Sunday

sonst else; **sonst noch
   etwas?** anything else?
sonstiges other items
Souvenir(s), n. souvenir
Spanien n. Spain
spanisch Spanish
spät late; **zu spät** too late
Spätzle(–), n. type of pasta
   popular in Swabia
spazieren gehen to go for a
   walk; **ich gehe spazieren** I'm
   going for a walk
Speise(n), f. food, dish
Speisekarte(n), f. menu
Spezialität(en), f. specialty
speziell special
Spiel(e), n. game, play
spielen to play; **Fußball
   spielen** to play soccer
Spielzeug(e), n. toy
Sport m. sport
sportlich sporty, casual (clothes)
Spottfigur(en), f. figure of fun
Sprache(n), f. language
Spray(s), n. spray
sprechen to speak
Stadt(¨e), f. town, city
Stadthalle municipal hall
städtisch municipal
Start(s), m. start, take off
starten to start, to take off
Station(en), f. stop
Stecken(–), m. stick (South
   German)
stehen to stand
Stein(e), m. stone
Stelle(n), f. post, job
sterben to die
Stern(e), m. star
still quiet
stimmt so keep the change
Stock (Stockwerke), n. floor,
   storey
Strand(¨), m. beach
Straße(n), f. street
Straßenbahn(en), f. tram
Streifenkarte(n), f. ticket for
   several trips
Stück(e), n. play, piece;
   ein Stück Kuchen a piece of
   cake; **ein modernes Stück** a
   modern play
Stunde(n), f. hour
stürzen to fall
Süden m. south; **im Süden** in
   the South; **in den Süden** to
   the South, south
Supermarkt(¨e), m. supermarket

Suppe(n), f. soup
süß sweet
süßlich sweetish

Tablette(n), f. tablet, pill
Tag(e), m. day
Tagessuppe(n), f. soup of the day
Tagestour(en), f. day trip
täglich daily
tanzen to dance
Tanzlokal(e), n. dance hall
Tarifzone(n), f. fare stage
Taschentuch(¨er), n. handkerchief
Tasse(n), f. cup
Taxi(s), n. taxi
TEE *Trans Europ Express* (Train)
Tee m. tea
Teewurst(¨e), f. smoked sausage
  spread
Teil(e), m. part; **zum Teil** partly
teuer expensive
Theater(-), n. theatre
Tiefstwert(e), m. lowest
  temperature
Tier(e), n. animal
Toast(s), m. toast
Tochter(÷), f. daughter
toll super, terrific
Tomate(n), f. tomato
Topf(¨e), m. pot
Torte(n), f. cake
tragisch tragic
Traum(¨e), m. dream
treffen to meet
trennen to divide
Tribüne(n), f. stand
Trimm-Dich-Pfad(e), m. keep-fit
  trail
trinken to drink
trocken dry
trotzdem nevertheless
tschüß (colloquial) good-bye
Turnier(e), n. tournament
typisch typical

U-Bahn(en), m. subway
über via, over
überall everywhere
überhaupt at all
Uhr(en), f. watch, clock; **um 6
  Uhr** at 6 o'clock
Umleitung(en), f. diversion
umsteigen to change (trains, buses)
umwechseln (or **wechseln**) to
  change (money)
umziehen to move
und and; **und so weiter** and so on
ungefähr approximately

ungewiß uncertain
unglücklich unhappy
Universität(en), f. university
unklar unclear
unter under, below; **unter
  Null** below zero
Unterführung(en), f. underpass
unterrichten to teach
unternehmen to do, to undertake
Urlaub(e), m. holiday; **im
  Urlaub** on holiday

verbannen to ban
Verbindung(en), f. connection
verbringen to spend
vereinzelt occasional
vereist icy
vergessen to forget
verheiratet married
verkaufen to sell
Verkäufer(-), m. shop assistant,
  m; **Verkäuferin(nen)**, f. shop
  assistant, f.
Verkehrbüro(s), n. tourist office
verkehren to run (between places)
vermissen to miss
verschieden various
verstehen to understand
Vertrag(¨e), m. contract
viel much, many; **vielen
  Dank** many thanks
vielleicht perhaps
vier four
Viertel(-), n. quarter; **Viertel nach
  vier** a quarter past four
voll full
Vollmilch f. milk (unskimmed)
volltanken to fill up (the tank)
von of, from
vor in front of
vor allem above all
vorher before that
Vorhersage(n), f. forecast
vorläufig in the near future
Vorname(n), m. first name
Vorort(e), m. suburb
Vorsicht f. attention, caution

wahrscheinlich probably
Wald(¨er), m. wood, forest
Waldlauf(¨e), m. (crosscountry)
  jogging
wandern to hike, to ramble
Wanderung(en), f. hiking tour
wann when
wäre: das wäre gut that would be
  good
warten to wait

warum why
was what; **was für Kuchen?** what
  kind of cake?
Wasser(–), n. water
Wechsel(–), m. change
wechselhaft changeable
wechseln to change
wecken to wake
Weg(e), m. way; path
weg away
weich soft
Weihnachten, n. Christmas
weil because
Wein(e), m. wine
weiß white
weiter further
welche,r,s which; **welcher
  Tag?** which day?
Welle(n), f. wave
Welt(en), f. world
wenig few
werden to become, to get; **es wird
  dunkel** it's getting dark; **ich
  werde gehen** I'll go
wesentlich substantially
Westen, m. west;
  Westdeutschland West Germany
Wetter n. weather
wichtig important
wie how; **wie geht's?** how are
  things?
wieder again
(Auf) Wiederschauen good-bye
  (South German)
(Auf) Wiederschen good bye
wieviel how much, how many
Wild n. venison, game
Willkommen n. welcome
Winter (–), m. winter
wir we
wirklich really
Wirtschaft(en), f. inn
wissen to know
wo where
Woche(n), f. week
Wochenende(n), n. weekend
woher where from
wohin where (to)
wohnen to live
Wohnung(en), f. flat, apartment
Wolke(n), f. cloud
wolkig cloudy

Wolle(n), f. wool
Wort(¨er and –e), n. word
wünschen to wish
würde would
Wurst(¨e), f. sausage
Würstchen(–), n. small sausage
Würstchenbude(n), f. sausage
  stand

Zahn(¨e), m. tooth
Zahnpasta f. toothpaste
Zahnschmerzen (pl.) toothache
zart delicate
zehn ten
Zeit(en), f. time; **zur Zeit** at the
  moment/time
Zeitschrift(en), f. magazine
Zeitung(en), f. newspaper
Zentrum (Zentren), n. centre
ziemlich rather
Zimmer(–), n. room
Zinn m. pewter
zirka approximately
Zitrone(n), f. lemon
Zoo(s), m. zoo
zu shut
zu to; **zur Bank** to the bank; **zum
  Hauptbahnhof** to the main
  station
zu too; **zu groß** too big
zu Hause at home
zu zweit with someone else
Zucker m. sugar
Zug(¨e), m. train
Zukunft f. future
zumachen to shut
zurück back
zusammen together
Zuschlag(¨e), m. surcharge
zwar: und zwar and that is to say
zwei two
zweimal twice; **zweimal Bonn
  einfach** two one-way tickets to
  Bonn
zweite, r,s second
Zwiebel(n), f. onion
Zwiebelrostbraten(–) m. roast beef
  with onions
zwischen between
zwo two
zwölf twelve

Index

Grammar in the course

Useful addresses

German National Tourist Office
630 Fifth Ave.
New York, NY 10020
(212) 757-8570

Austrian National Tourist Office
545 Fifth Ave.
New York, NY 10017
(212) 737-6400

200 E. Randolph
Chicago, IL 60601
(312) 861-0103

Swiss National Tourist Office
608 Fifth Ave.
New York, NY 10020
(212) 757-5944

104 S. Michigan Ave.
Room 200
Chicago, IL 60603
(312) 641-0050

Deutscher Fremdenverkehrsverband
(German Tourist Association)
Beethovenstrasse 61
D – 6000 Frankfurt/Main

Deutscher Camping-Club
(German Camping Association)
Mandlstrasse 28
D – 8000 München 40

ADAC
(German Automobile Association)
Baumgartner Strasse 53
D – 8000 München 70

LANGUAGE AND REFERENCE BOOKS

Dictionaries and References
VOX Spanish and English Dictionaries
Cervantes-Walls Spanish and English Dictionary
Klett German and English Dictionary
NTC's New College French & English Dictionary
NTC's New College Greek & English Dictionary
Zanichelli New College Italian & English Dictionary
Zanichelli Super-Mini Italian & English Dictionary
NTC's Dictionary of Spanish False Cognates
NTC's Dictionary of German False Cognates
NTC's Dictionary of *Faux Amis*
NTC's American Idioms Dictionary
NTC's Dictionary of American Slang and
  Colloquial Expressions
Forbidden American English
Essential American Idioms
Contemporary American Slang
Everyday American English Dictionary
Everyday American Phrases in Content
Beginner's Dictionary of American English Usage
NTC's Dictionary of Grammar Terminology
Robin Hyman's Dictionary of Quotations
Guide to Better English Spelling
303 Dumb Spelling Mistakes
NTC's Dictionary of Literary Terms
The Writer's Handbook
Diccionario Inglés
El Diccionario Básico Norteamericano
British/American Language Dictionary
The French-Speaking World
The Spanish-Speaking World
Guide to Spanish Idioms
Guide to German Idioms
Guide to French Idioms
101 Japanese Idioms
Au courant
Guide to Correspondence in Spanish
Guide to Correspondence in French
Español para los Hispanos
Business Russian
Yes! You Can Learn a Foreign Language
Japanese in Plain English
Korean in Plain English
Easy Chinese Phrasebook and Dictionary
Japan Today!
Everything Japanese
Easy Hiragana
Easy Katakana
Easy Kana Workbook
The Wiedza Powszechna Compact Polish & English
  Dictionary

Picture Dictionaries
English; French; Spanish; German

Let's Learn...Picture Dictionaries
English, Spanish, French, German, Italian

Verb References
Complete Handbook of Spanish Verbs
Complete Handbook of Russian Verbs
Spanish Verb Drills
French Verb Drills
German Verb Drills

Grammar References
Spanish Verbs and Essentials of Grammar
Nice 'n Easy Spanish Grammar
French Verbs and Essentials of Grammar
Real French
Nice 'n Easy French Grammar
German Verbs and Essentials of Grammar
Nice 'n Easy German Grammar
Italian Verbs and Essentials of Grammar
Essentials of Russian Grammar
Essentials of English Grammar
Roots of the Russian Language
Reading and Translating Contemporary Russian
Essentials of Latin Grammar
Swedish Verbs and Essentials of Grammar

Welcome to...Books
Spain, France, Ancient Greece, Ancient Rome

Language Programs: Audio and Video
Just Listen 'n Learn: Spanish, French, Italian, German,
  Greek
Just Listen 'n Learn PLUS: Spanish, French, German
Speak French
Speak Spanish
Speak German
Practice & Improve Your...Spanish, French, Italian,
  German
Practice & Improve Your...Spanish PLUS, French PLUS,
  Italian PLUS, German PLUS
Improve Your...Spanish, French, Italian, German: The
  P & I Method
Conversational...in 7 Days: Spanish, French, German,
  Italian, Portuguese, Greek, Russian, Japanese, Thai
Everyday Japanese
Japanese for Children
Nissan's Business Japanese
Contemporary Business Japanese
Basic French Conversation
Basic Spanish Conversation
Everyday Hebrew
VideoPassport in French and Spanish
How to Pronounce Russian Correctly
How to Pronounce Spanish Correctly
How to Pronounce French Correctly
How to Pronounce Italian Correctly
How to Pronounce Japanese Correctly
L'Express: Ainsi va la France
L'Express: Aujourd'hui la France
Der Spiegel: Aktuelle Themen in der Bundesrepublik
  Deutschland
Listen and Say It Right in English
Once Upon a Time in Spanish, French, German
Let's Sing & Learn in French & Spanish

"Just Enough" Phrase Books
Chinese, Dutch, French, German, Greek, Hebrew,
  Hungarian, Italian, Japanese, Portuguese, Russian,
  Scandinavian, Serbo-Croat, Spanish
Business French, Business German, Business Spanish

Language Game and Humor Books
Easy French Vocabulary Games
Easy French Crossword Puzzles
Easy French Word Games and Puzzles
Easy French Grammar Puzzles
Easy Spanish Word Power Games
Easy Spanish Crossword Puzzles
Easy Spanish Vocabulary Puzzles
Easy French Word Games and Puzzles
Easy French Culture Games
Easy German Crossword Puzzles
Easy Italian Crossword Puzzles
Let's Learn about Series: Italy, France, Germany, Spain,
  America
Let's Learn Coloring Books in Spanish, French, German,
  Italian, English
Let's Learn...Spanish, French, German, Italian, English
  Coloring Book-Audiocassette Package
My World in...Coloring Books: Spanish, French,
  German, Italian
German à la Cartoon
Spanish à la Cartoon
French à la Cartoon
101 American English Idioms
El alfabeto
L'alphabet

Getting Started Books
Introductory language books in Spanish, French,
  German, Italian

Ticket to...Series
France, Germany, Spain, Italy (Guide and audiocassette)

Getting to Know...Series
France, Germany, Spain, Italy,
  Mexico, United States

PASSPORT BOOKS
a division of *NTC Publishing Group*
Lincolnwood, Illinois USA